MONOLOGUES FOR THE COMING PLAGUE

anders nilsen

fantagraphics books

introduction

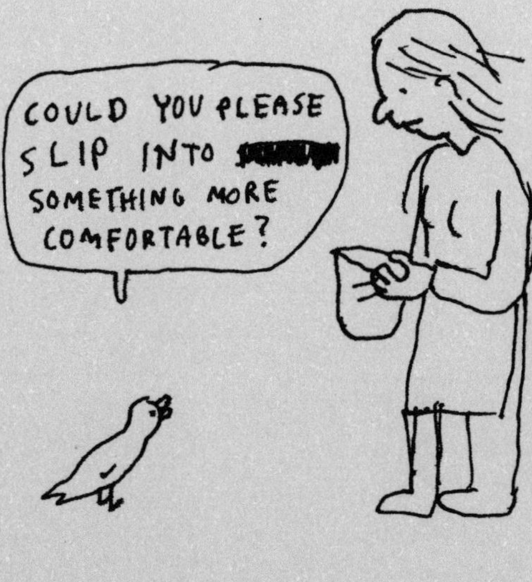
COULD YOU PLEASE SLIP INTO [redacted] SOMETHING MORE COMFORTABLE?

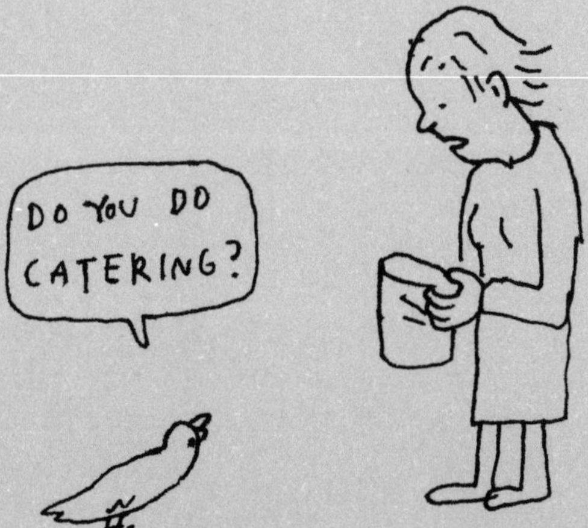
DO YOU DO CATERING?

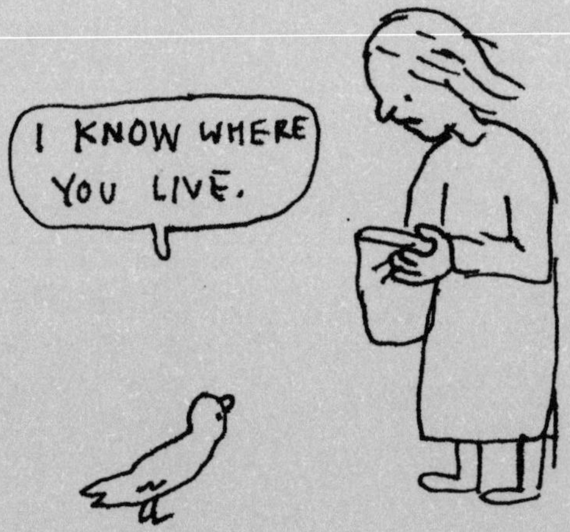
I KNOW WHERE YOU LIVE.

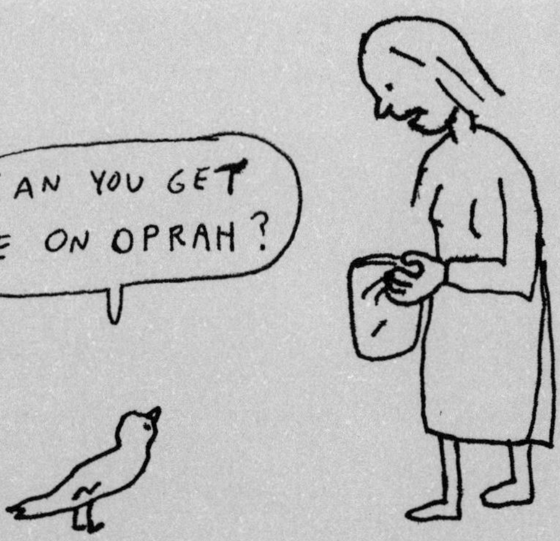
CAN YOU GET ME ON OPRAH?

YOU'RE FIRED

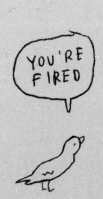

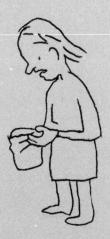

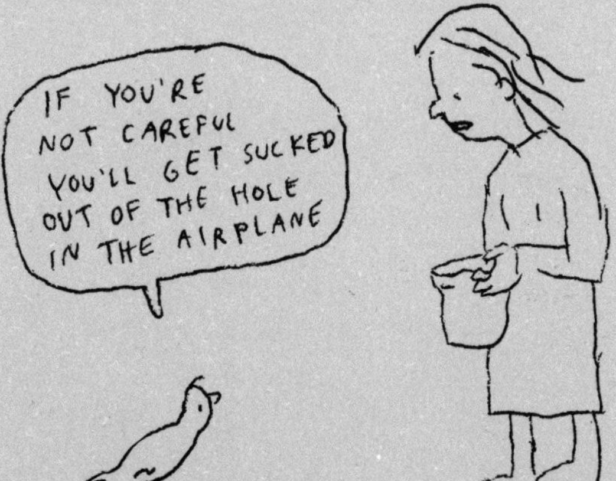
IF YOU'RE NOT CAREFUL YOU'LL GET SUCKED OUT OF THE HOLE IN THE AIRPLANE

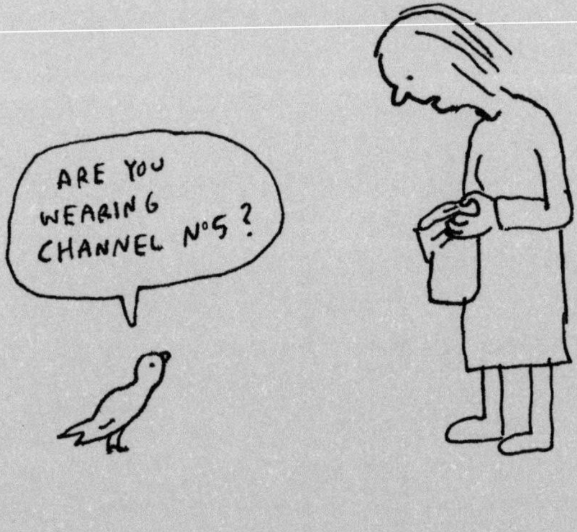
ARE YOU WEARING CHANNEL Nº5?

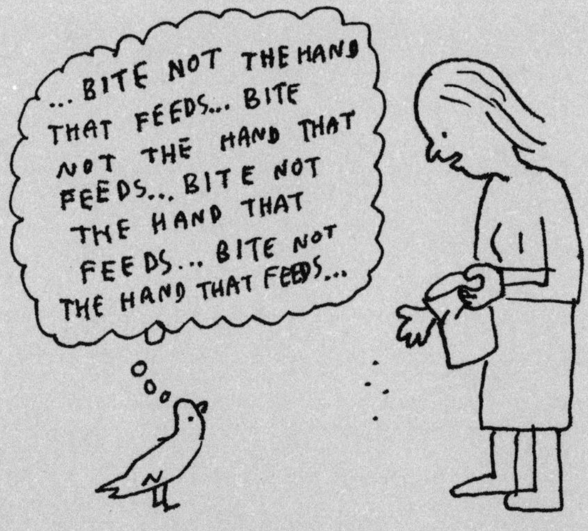
... BITE NOT THE HAND THAT FEEDS... BITE NOT THE HAND THAT FEEDS... BITE NOT THE HAND THAT FEEDS... BITE NOT THE HAND THAT FEEDS...

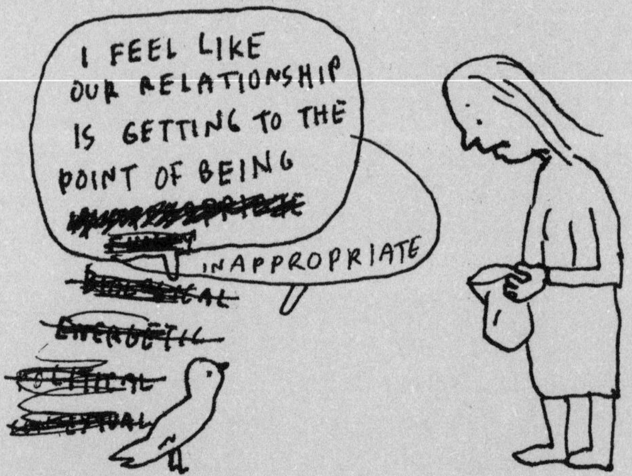
I FEEL LIKE OUR RELATIONSHIP IS GETTING TO THE POINT OF BEING
INAPPROPRIATE
ENERGETIC
FERMENTED

I THINK IT'S TIME YOU STOPPED BLAMING EVERYTHING ON YOUR PARENTS AND JUST SUCK IT UP.

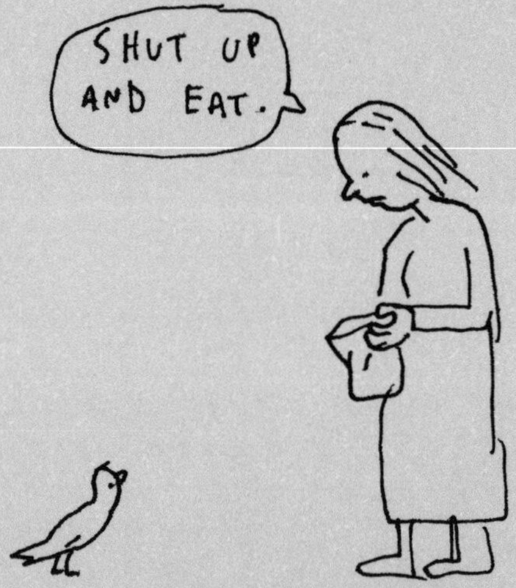
SHUT UP AND EAT.

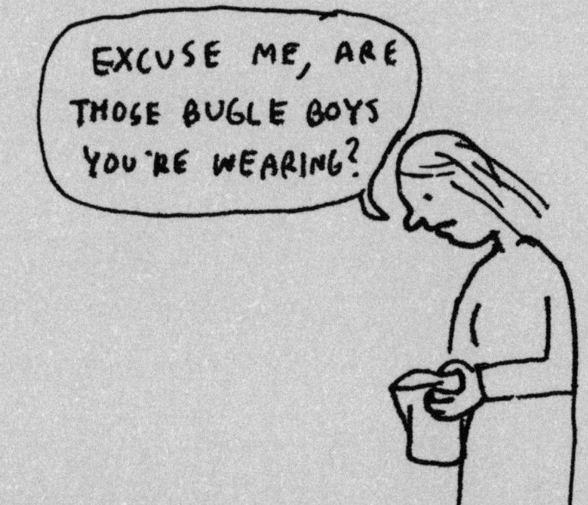
EXCUSE ME, ARE THOSE BUGLE BOYS YOU'RE WEARING?

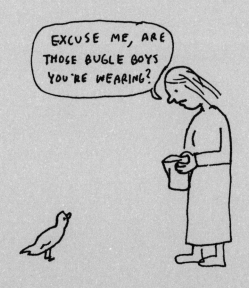

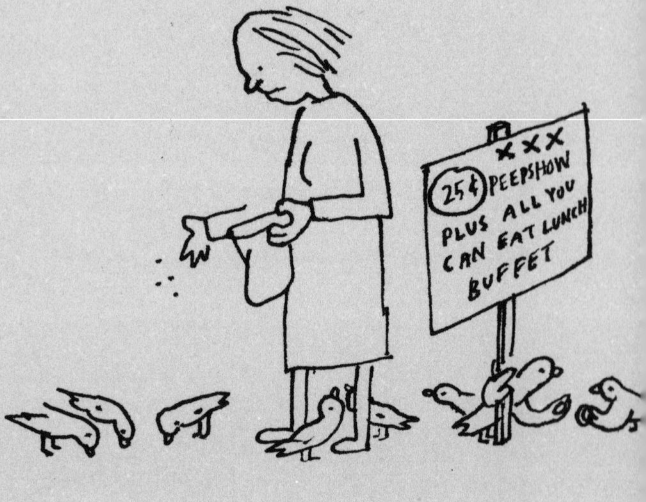
XXX
25¢ PEEPSHOW
PLUS ALL YOU
CAN EAT LUNCH
BUFFET

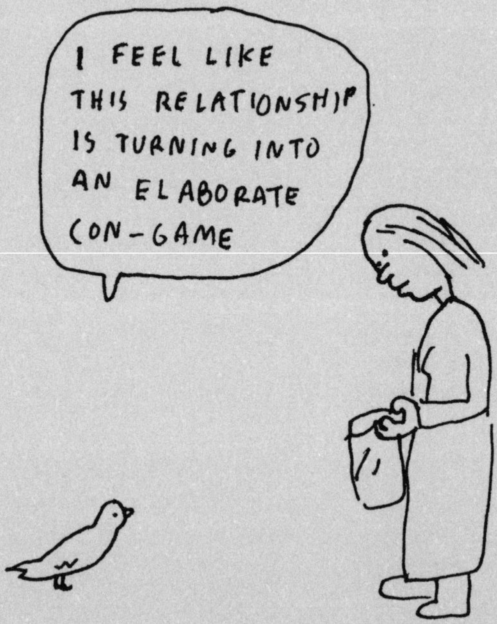
I FEEL LIKE THIS RELATIONSHIP IS TURNING INTO AN ELABORATE CON-GAME

semiotics

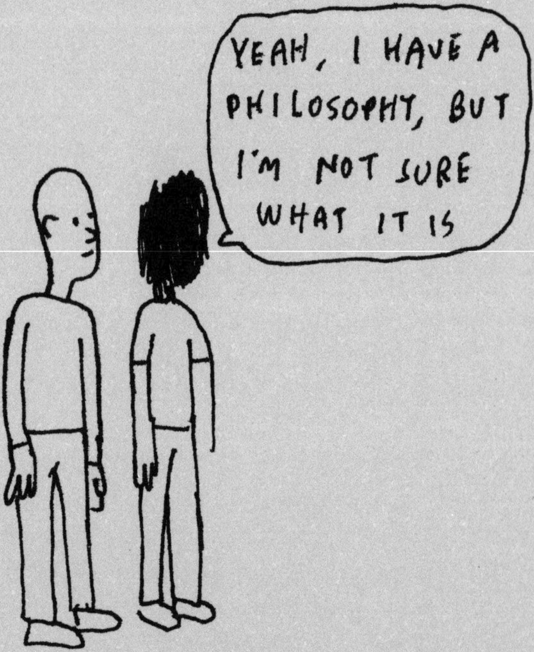
YEAH, I HAVE A PHILOSOPHY, BUT I'M NOT SURE WHAT IT IS

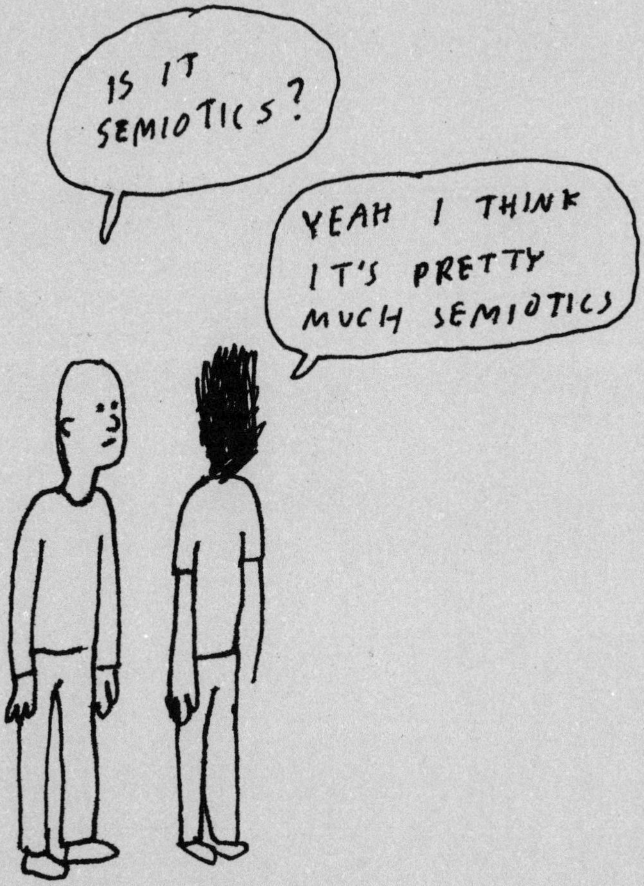
IS IT SEMIOTICS?
YEAH I THINK IT'S PRETTY MUCH SEMIOTICS

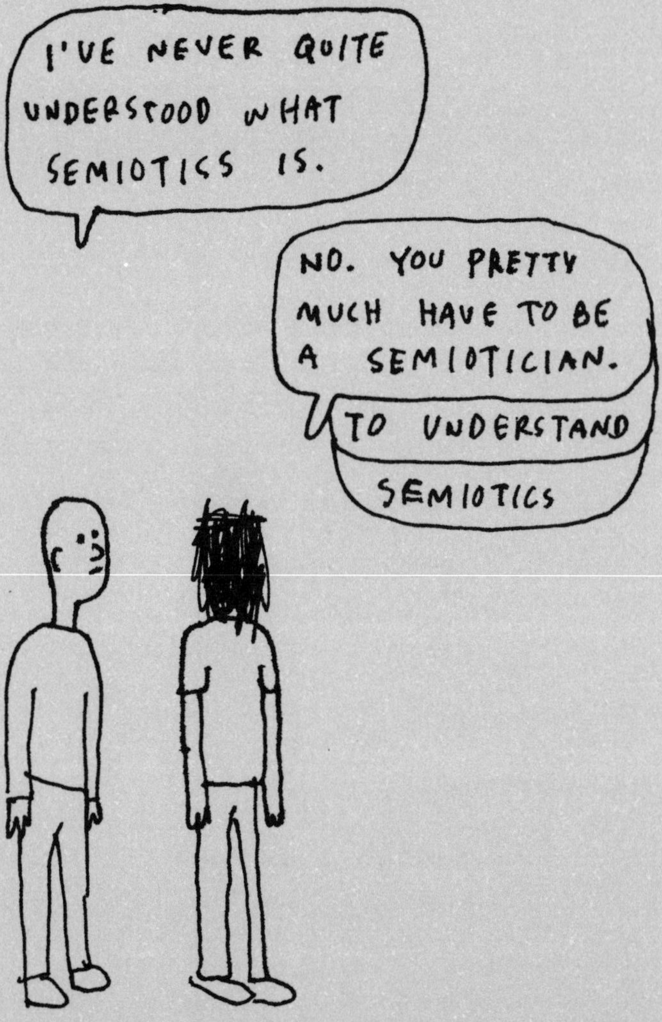
I'VE NEVER QUITE UNDERSTOOD WHAT SEMIOTICS IS.
NO. YOU PRETTY MUCH HAVE TO BE A SEMIOTICIAN.
TO UNDERSTAND
SEMIOTICS

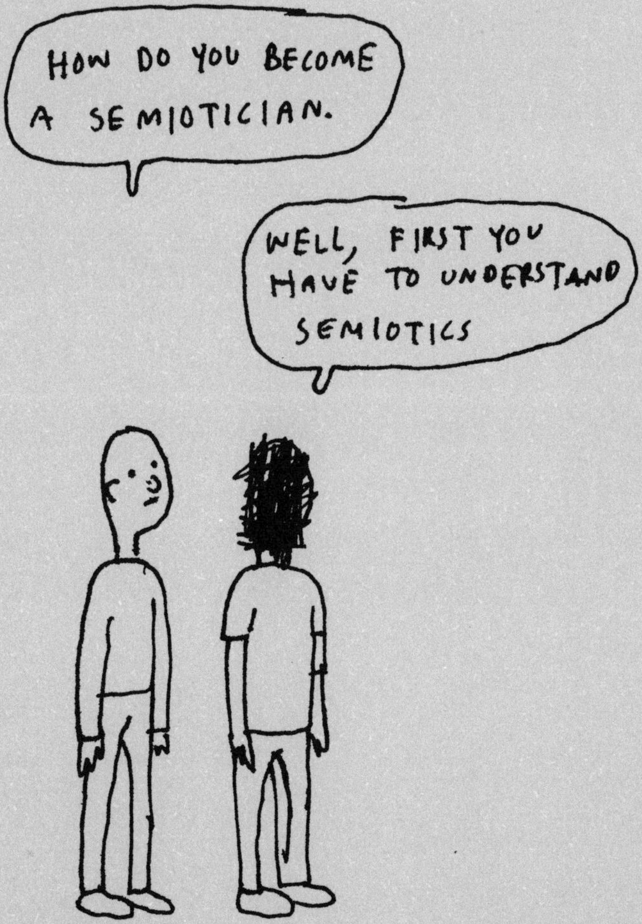
HOW DO YOU BECOME A SEMIOTICIAN.
WELL, FIRST YOU HAVE TO UNDERSTAND SEMIOTICS

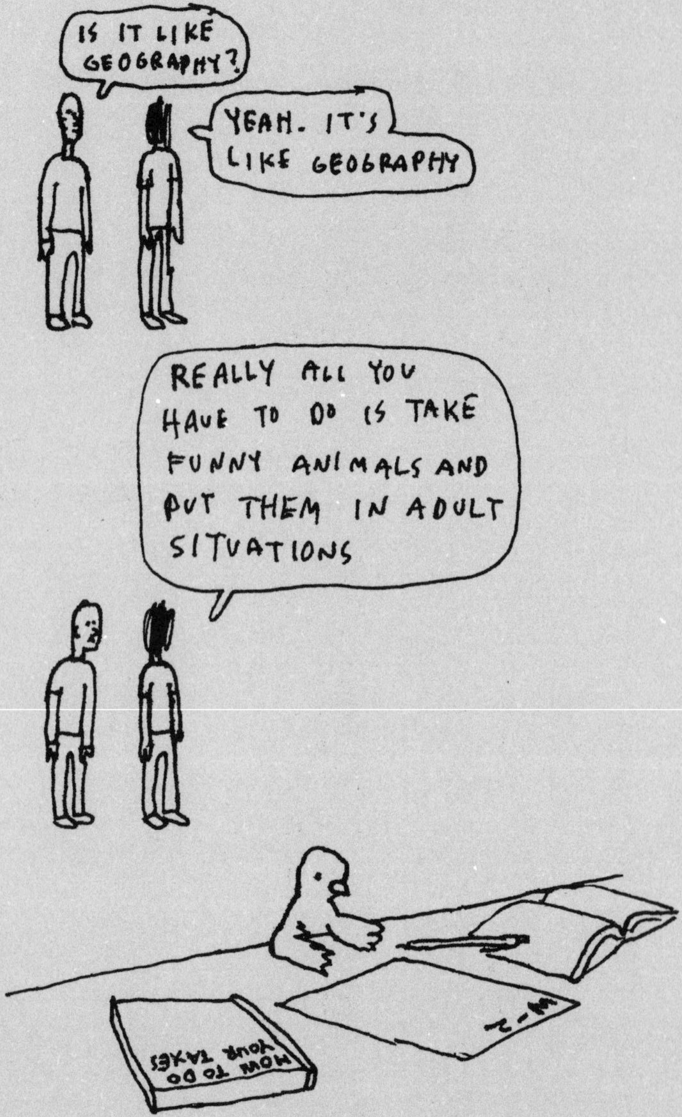
IS IT LIKE GEOGRAPHY?
YEAH. IT'S LIKE GEOGRAPHY
REALLY ALL YOU HAVE TO DO IS TAKE FUNNY ANIMALS AND PUT THEM IN ADULT SITUATIONS
HOW TO DO YOUR TAXES

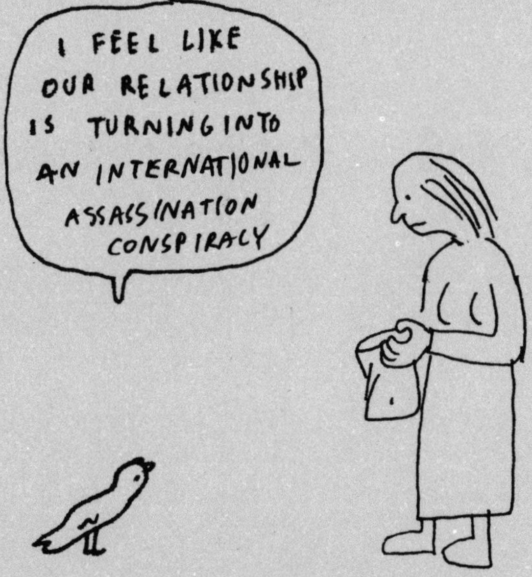
I FEEL LIKE OUR RELATIONSHIP IS TURNING INTO AN INTERNATIONAL ASSASSINATION CONSPIRACY

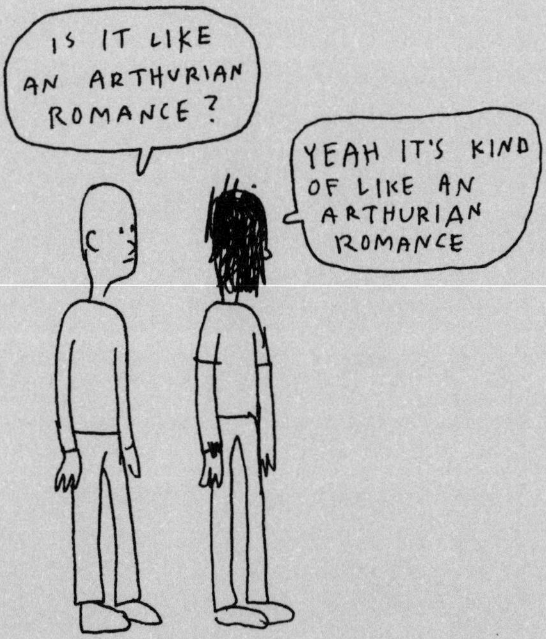
IS IT LIKE AN ARTHURIAN ROMANCE?
YEAH IT'S KIND OF LIKE AN ARTHURIAN ROMANCE

IS IT LIKE MODERN CLASSICAL MUSIC ?
YEAH, IT'S SORT OF LIKE MODERN CLASSICAL MUSIC

IS IT LIKE, WHAM-BAM-THANK YOU MA'AM?

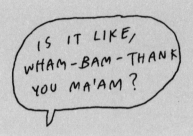

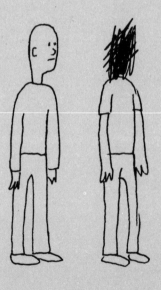

HAVE YOU HEARD
ANY OF TUPAC'S
MUSIC SINCE HE
DIED?

~~IT ALL SOUNDS~~
~~THE SAME.~~

HE HASN'T
GROWN AT ALL
MUSICALLY.

WHAT DOESN'T
KILL YOU MAKES
YOU STRINGIER

I'M STILL NOT SURE I UNDERSTAND THIS "SEMIOTICS"

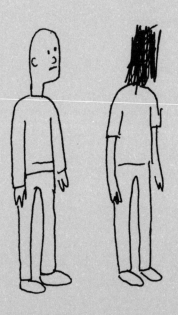

MAYBE YOU SHOULD TAKE SOME GRADUATE COURSES IN ECONOMICS

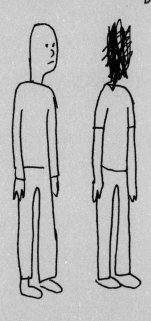

FOR EXAMPLE, LET'S TAKE THIS SENTENCE APART AND SEE WHAT WE GET
WHAM BAM THANK YOU MA'AM

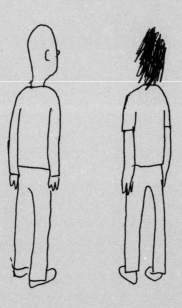

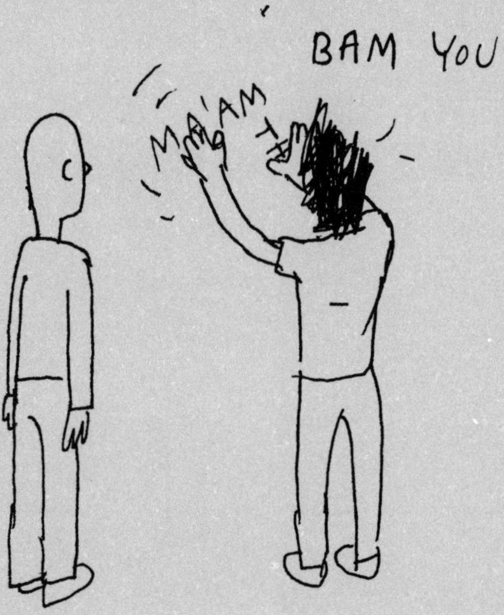
BAM YOU

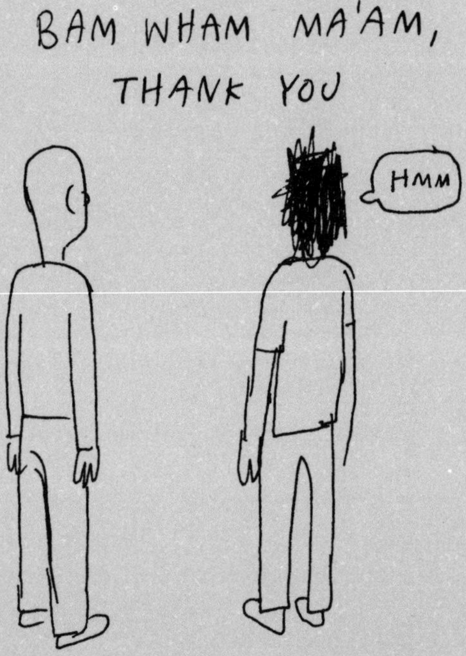
BAM WHAM MA'AM,
THANK YOU
HMM

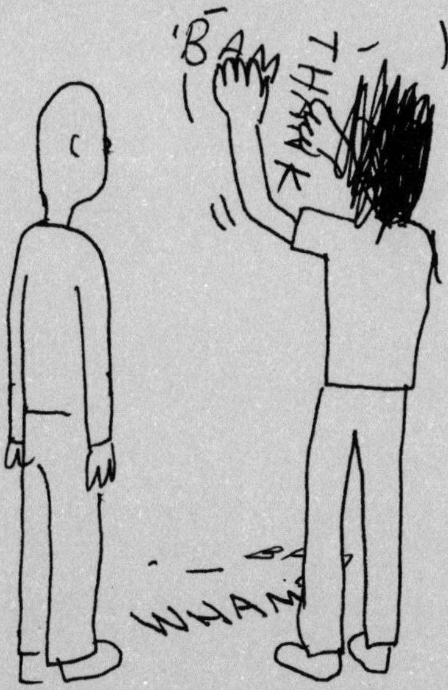
BAM
THWACK
WHAM

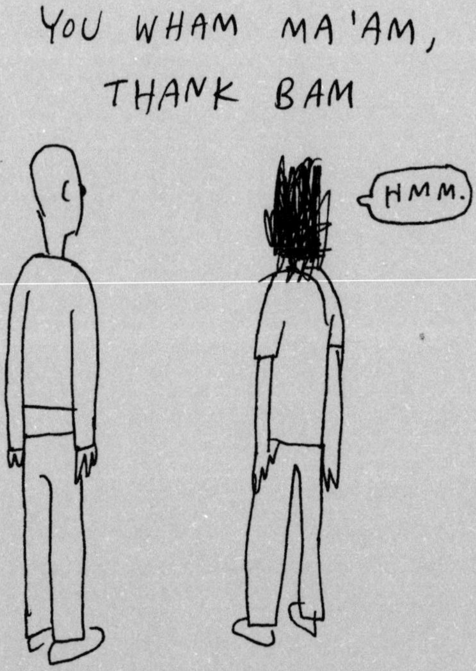
YOU WHAM MA'AM,
THANK BAM
HMM.

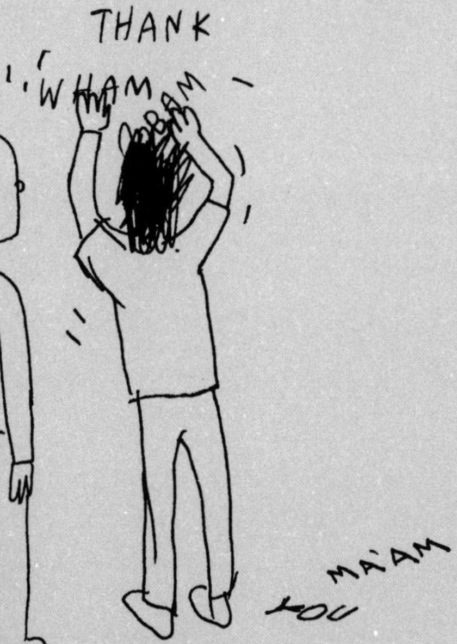
THANK
WHAM
BAM
MA'AM
YOU

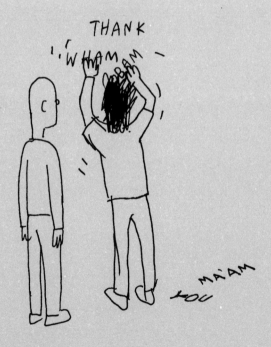

THANK BAM, MA'AM

WHAM YOU

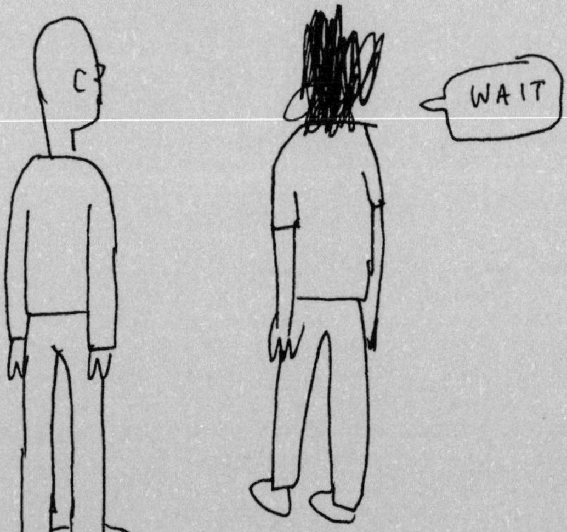
WAIT

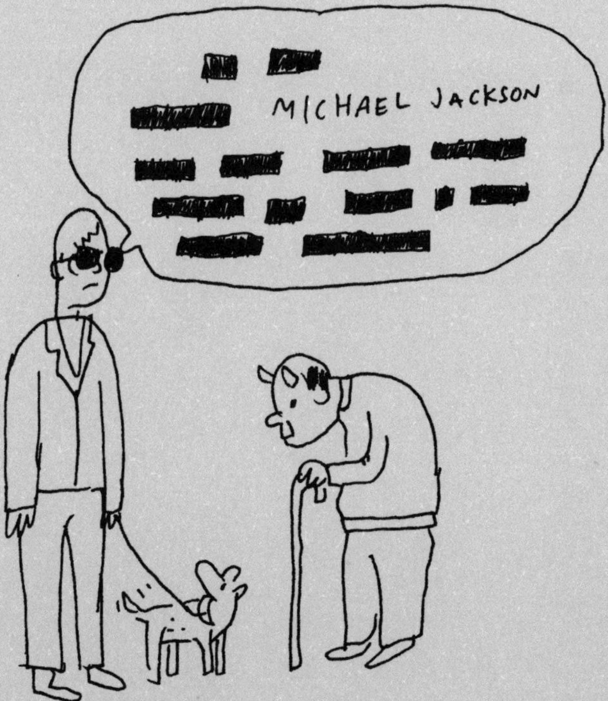
[redacted] MICHAEL JACKSON [redacted]

THANK BAM, MA'AM
WHAM YOU

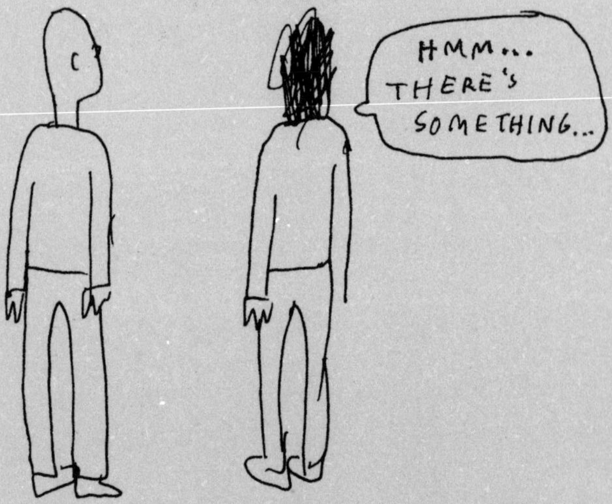
HMM... THERE'S SOMETHING...

THANK BAM, MA'AM
WHAM YOU

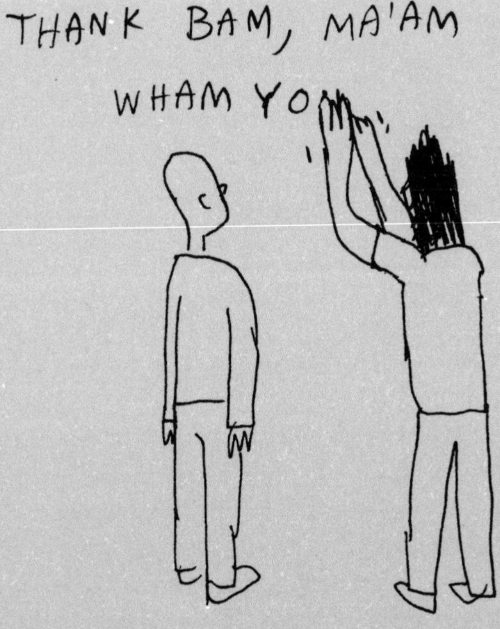
THANK BAM, MA'AM
WHAM YO

THANK BAM, MA'AM

WHAM YOU ?

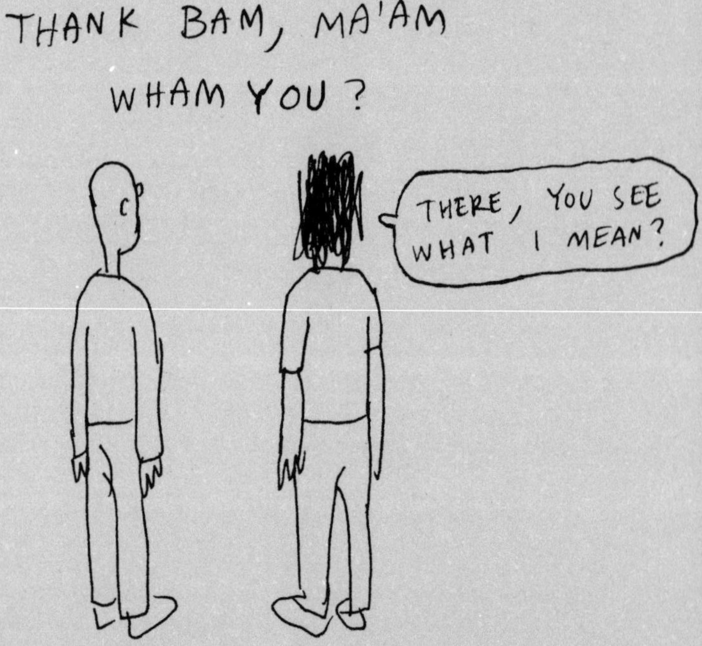
THANK BAM, MA'AM
WHAM YOU?
THERE, YOU SEE WHAT I MEAN?

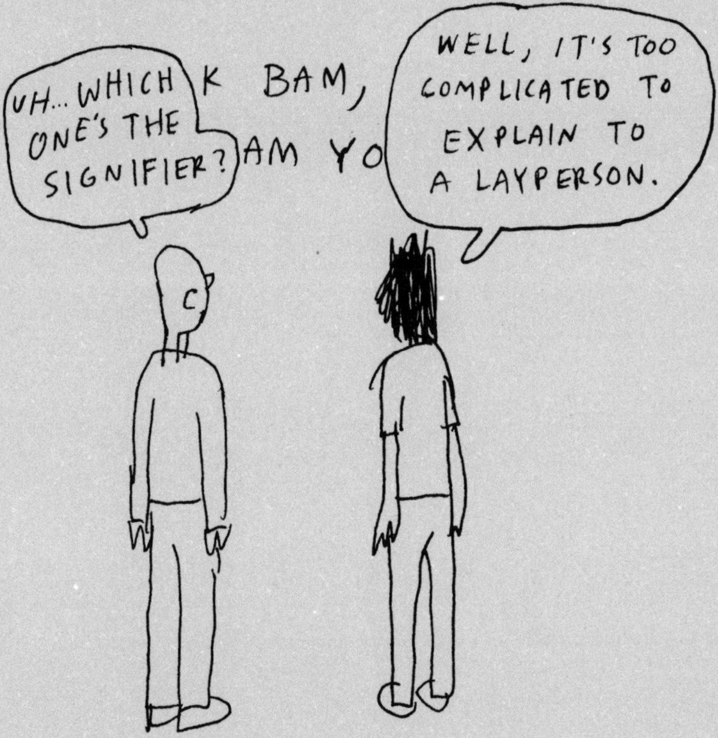
UH... WHICH ONE'S THE SIGNIFIER?
K BAM,
AM YO
WELL, IT'S TOO COMPLICATED TO EXPLAIN TO A LAYPERSON.

THANK BAM MA'AM
WHAM YOU ?

THANK BAM, MA'AM
WHAM YOU ?

BAMAAM

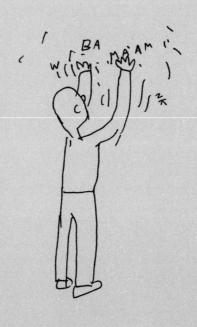

TKBHAAA
MMHOU
MNYAAA

TKBHAAA
MMHOU
MNYAAA

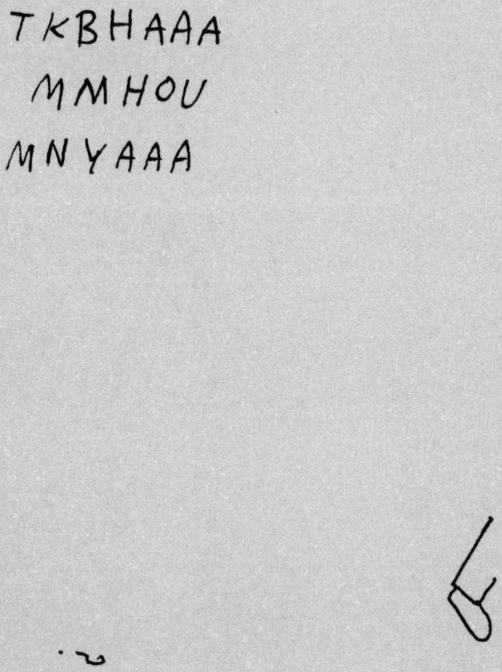

TKBHAAA
MMHOU
MNYAAA

FOR EXAMPLE, LET'S TAKE THIS SENTENCE APART AND SEE WHAT HAPPENS

NEW TIDE ULTRA BRIGHTENS AND WHITENS LIKE NEVER BEFORE!

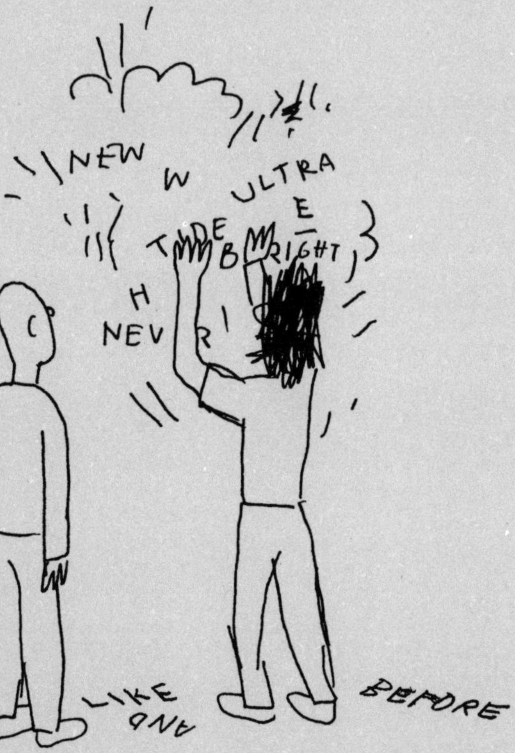
NEW
W
ULTRA
E
B
RIGHT
H
NEV
R
LIKE
AND
BEFORE

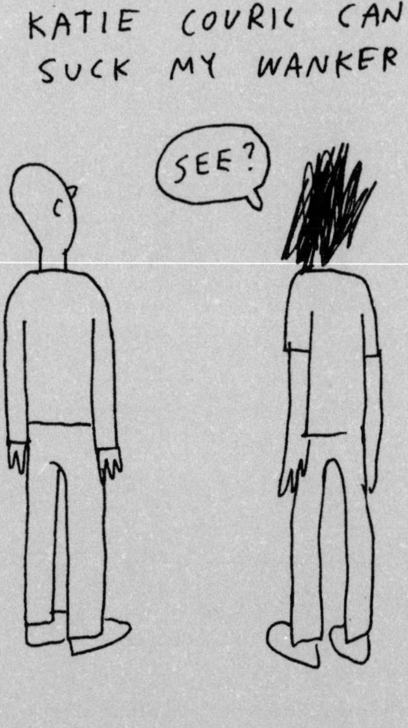
KATIE COURIC CAN SUCK MY WANKER
SEE?

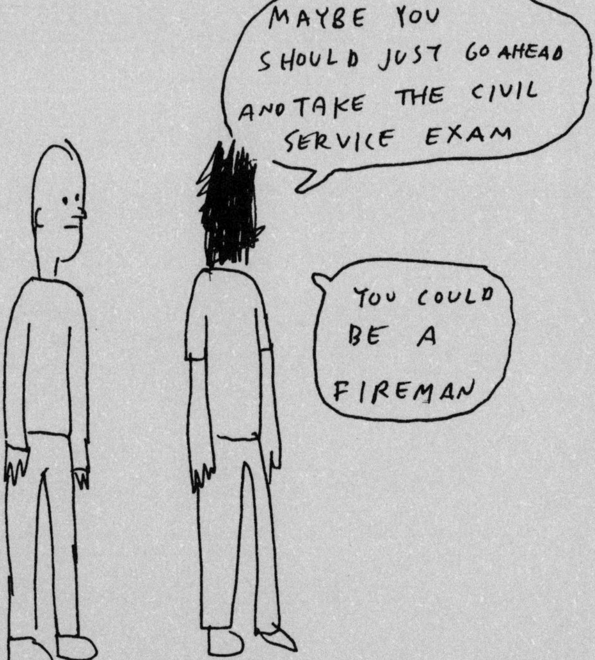
MAYBE YOU SHOULD JUST GO AHEAD AND TAKE THE CIVIL SERVICE EXAM
YOU COULD BE A FIREMAN

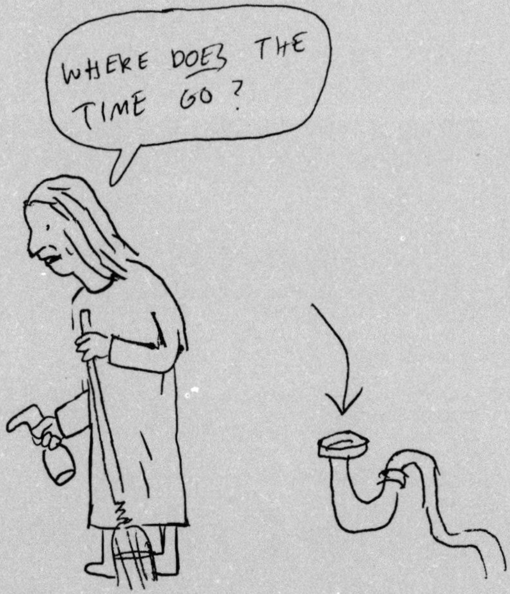
WHERE DOES THE TIME GO?

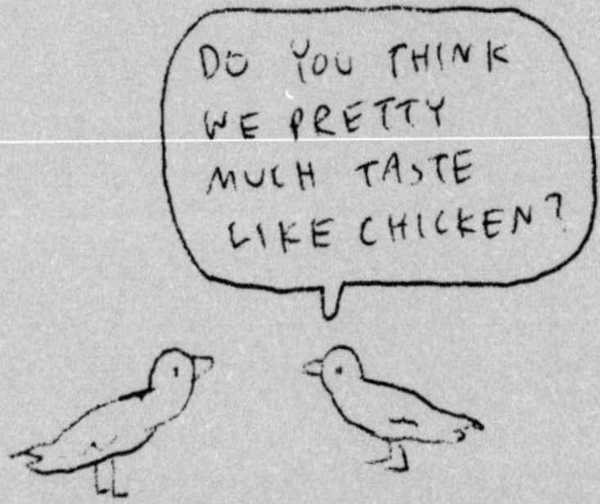
DO YOU THINK WE PRETTY MUCH TASTE LIKE CHICKEN?

pittsburgh

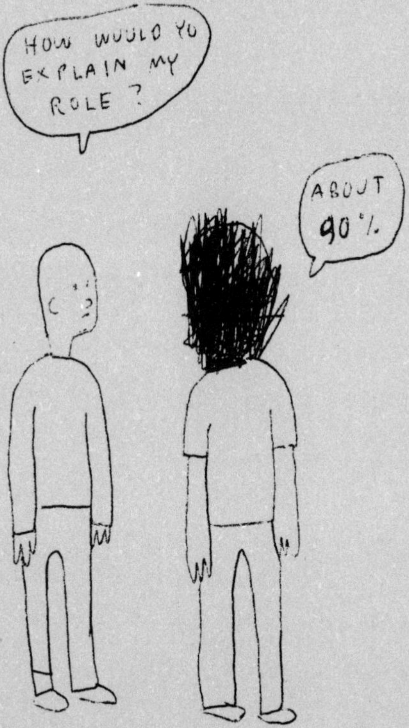
HOW WOULD YO EXPLAIN MY ROLE ?
ABOUT 90%

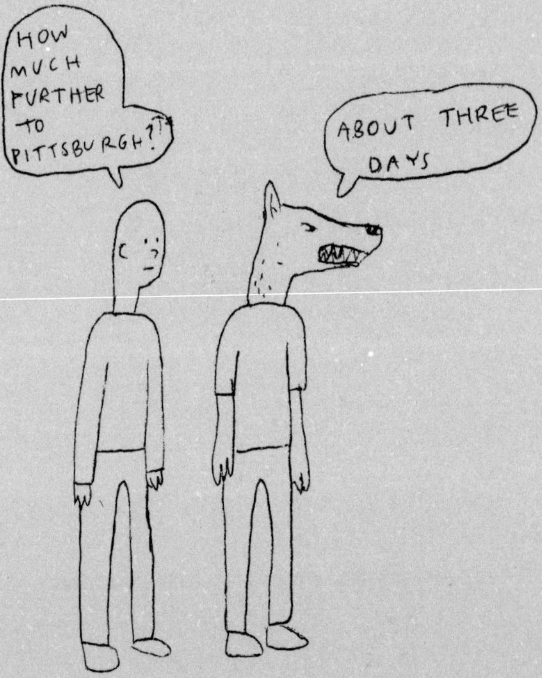
HOW MUCH FURTHER TO PITTSBURGH?
ABOUT THREE DAYS

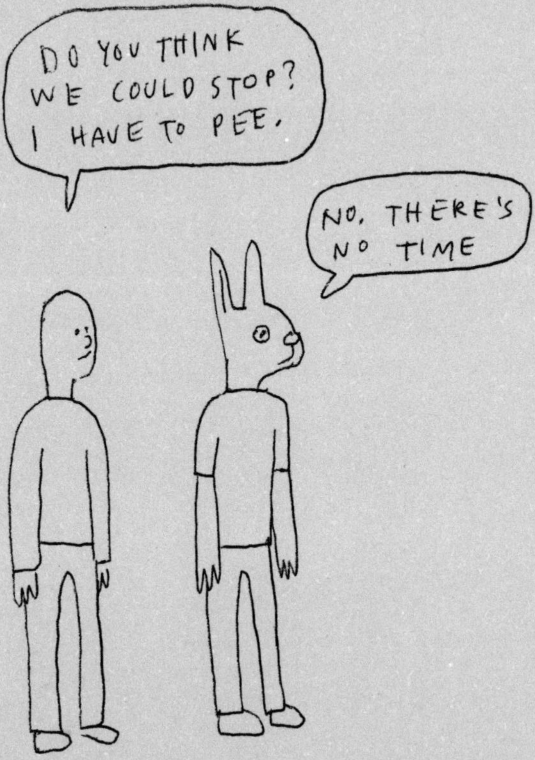
DO YOU THINK WE COULD STOP? I HAVE TO PEE.
NO. THERE'S NO TIME

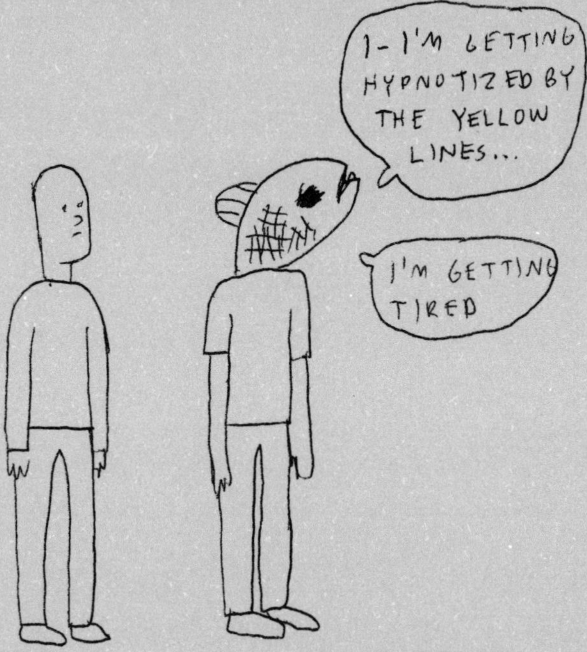
I-I'M GETTING HYPNOTIZED BY THE YELLOW LINES...
I'M GETTING TIRED

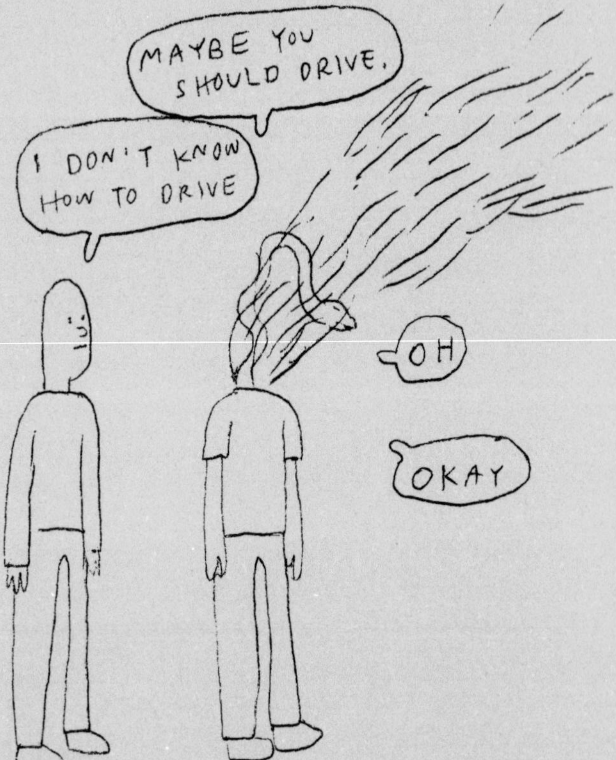
MAYBE YOU SHOULD DRIVE.
I DON'T KNOW HOW TO DRIVE
OH
OKAY

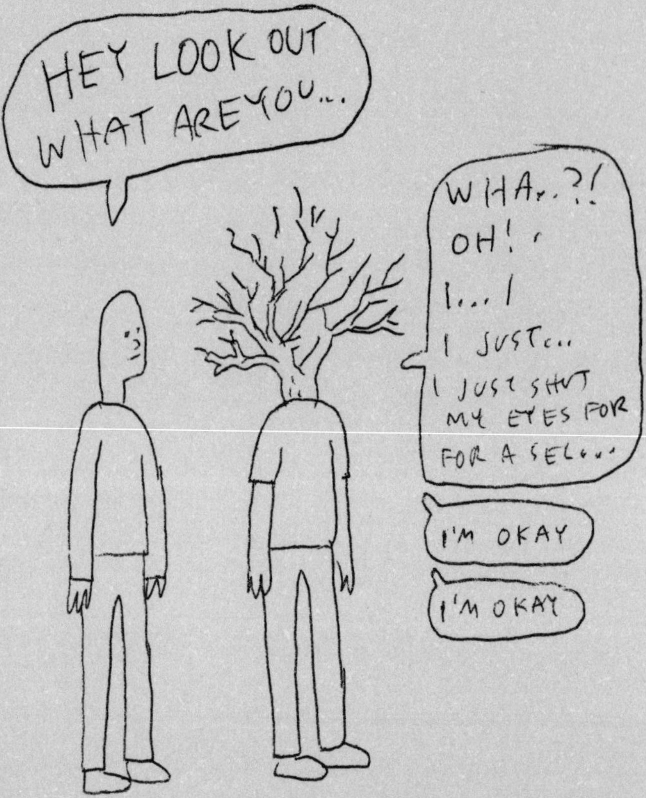
HEY LOOK OUT WHAT AREYOU...
WHA..?! OH! I...I I JUST... I JUST SHUT MY EYES FOR FOR A SEC...
I'M OKAY
I'M OKAY

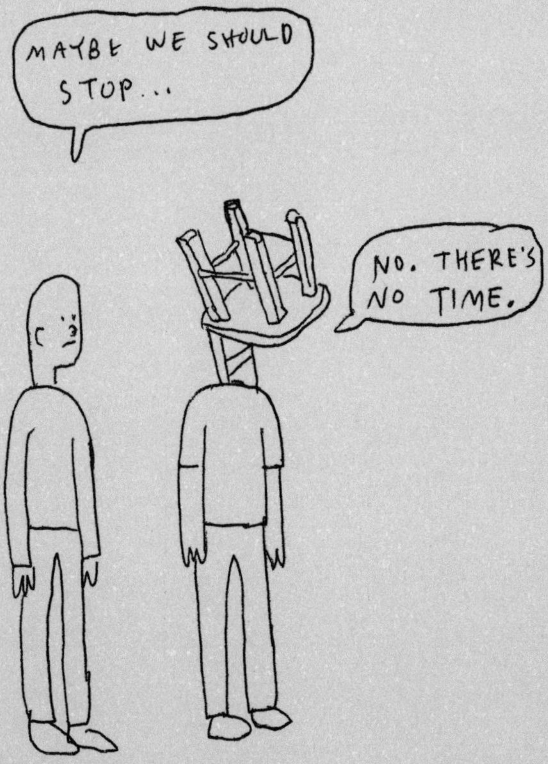
MAYBE WE SHOULD STOP...
NO. THERE'S NO TIME.

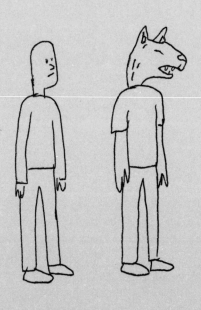

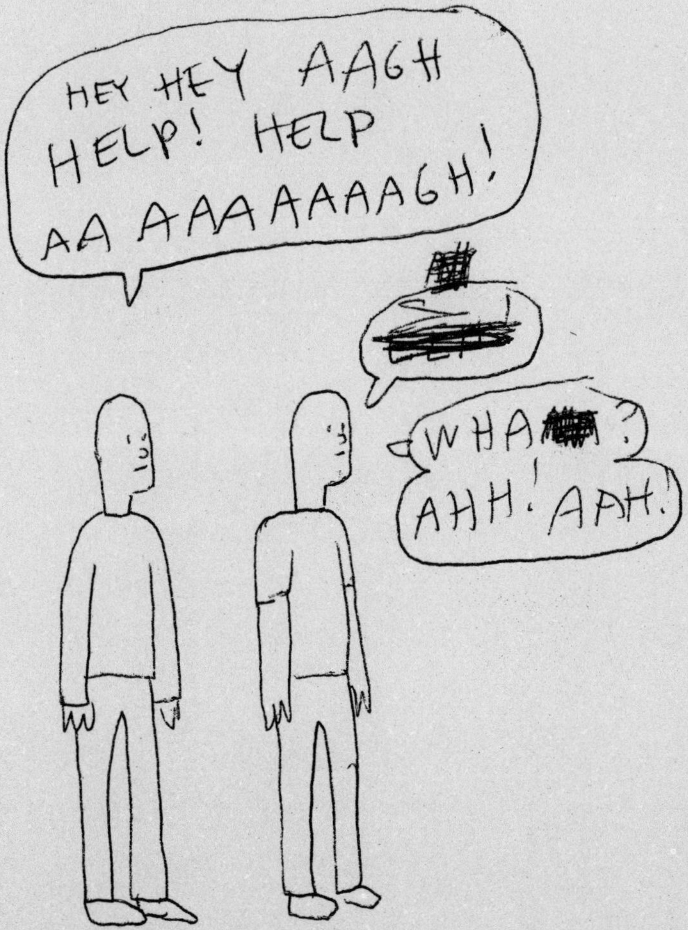
HEY HEY AAGH HELP! HELP AA AAAAAAAGH!
WHA ?
AHH! AAH!

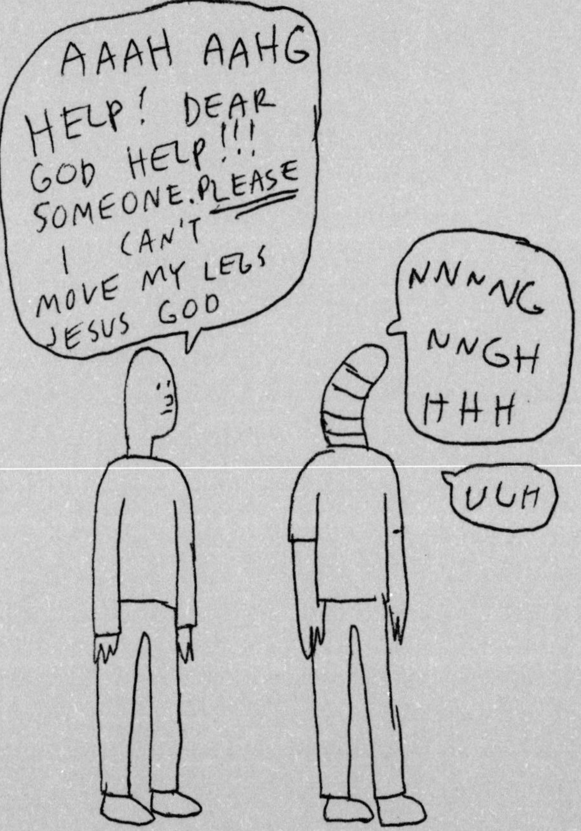
AAAH AAHG HELP! DEAR GOD HELP!!! SOMEONE. PLEASE I CAN'T MOVE MY LEGS JESUS GOD
NNNNNG NNGH HHH
UUH

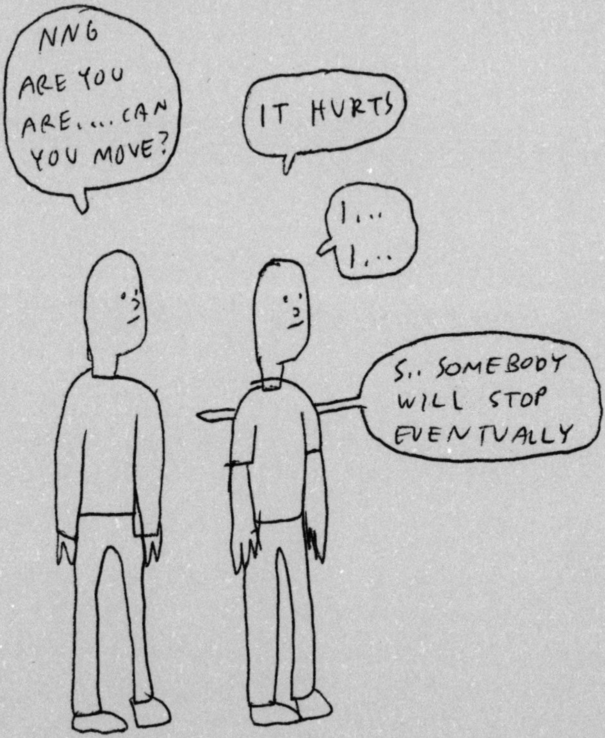
NNG
ARE YOU
ARE.....CAN
YOU MOVE?
IT HURTS
I...
I...
S.. SOMEBODY
WILL STOP
EVENTUALLY

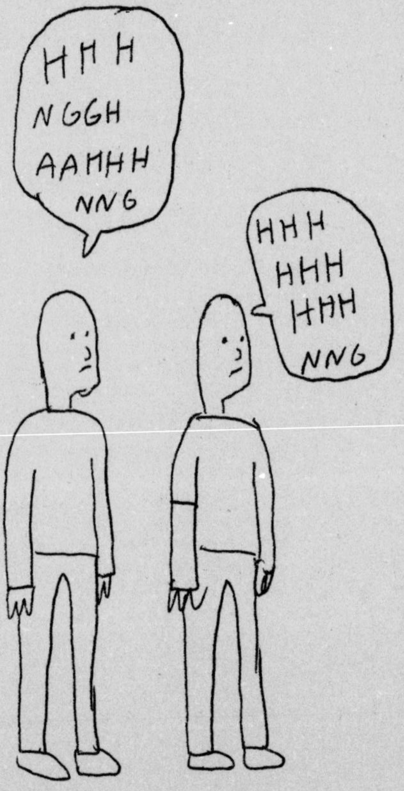
HHH
NGGH
AAHHH
NNG
HHH
HHH
HHH
NNG

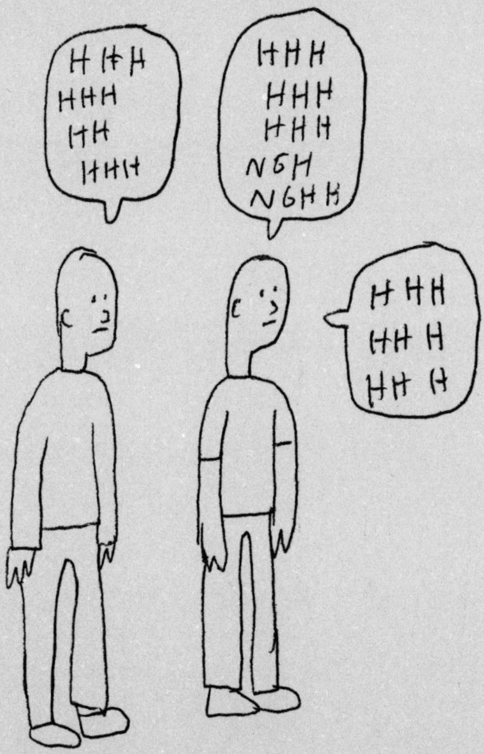
HHH
HHH
HH
HHH
HHH
HHH
HHH
NGH
NGHH
HHH
HHH
HH H

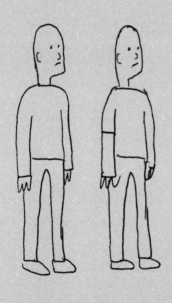

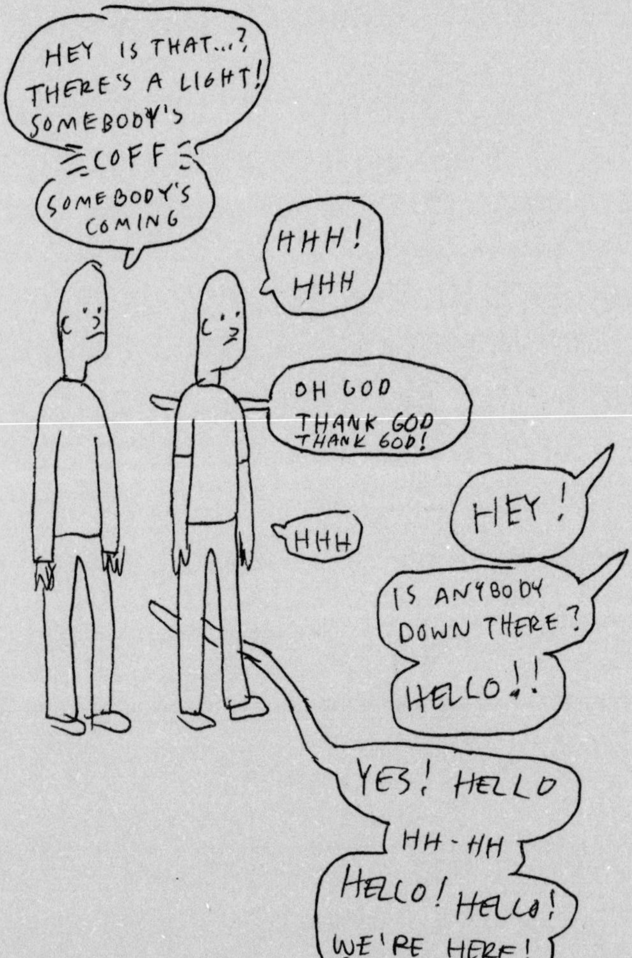

HEY IS THAT...? THERE'S A LIGHT! SOMEBODY'S
COFF
SOMEBODY'S COMING
HHH! HHH
OH GOD THANK GOD THANK GOD!
HHH
HEY!
IS ANYBODY DOWN THERE?
HELLO!!
YES! HELLO
HH-HH
HELLO! HELLO!
WE'RE HERE! OVER HERE!

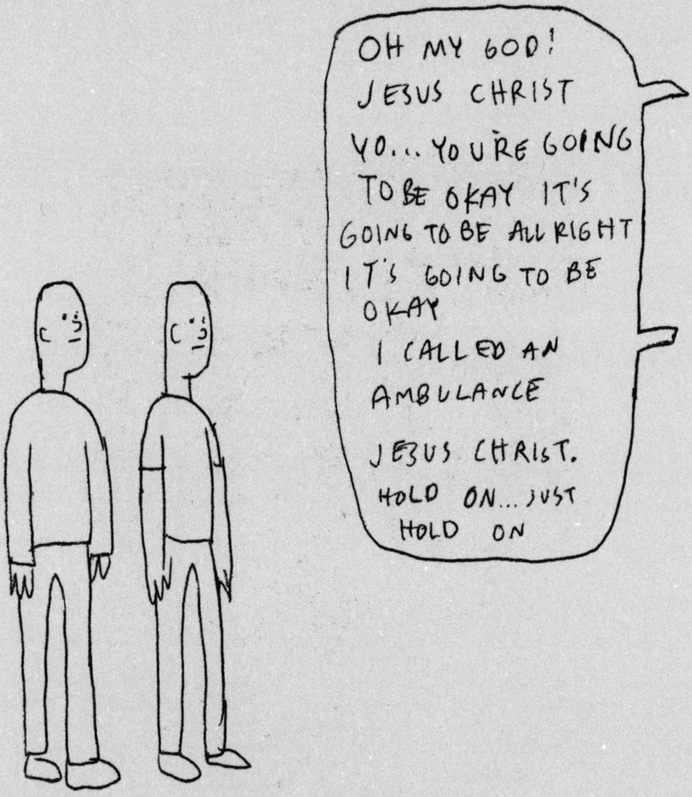
OH MY GOD!
JESUS CHRIST
YO... YOU'RE GOING TO BE OKAY IT'S GOING TO BE ALL RIGHT IT'S GOING TO BE OKAY
I CALLED AN AMBULANCE
JESUS CHRIST.
HOLD ON... JUST HOLD ON

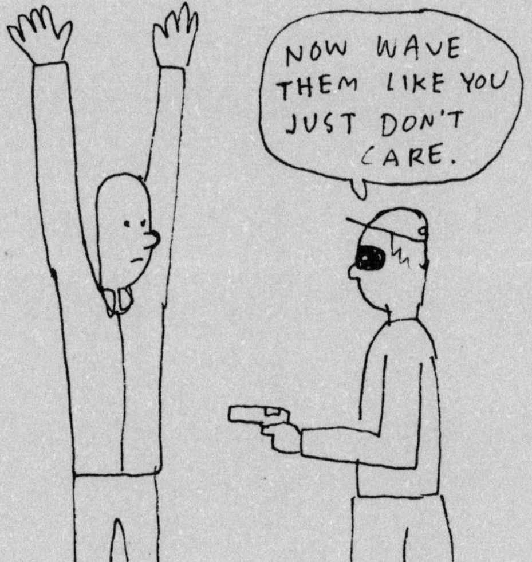
NOW WAVE THEM LIKE YOU JUST DON'T CARE.

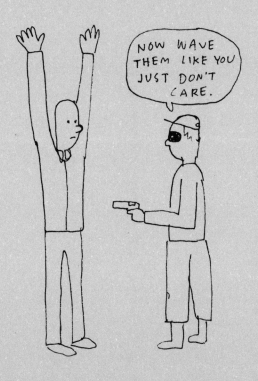

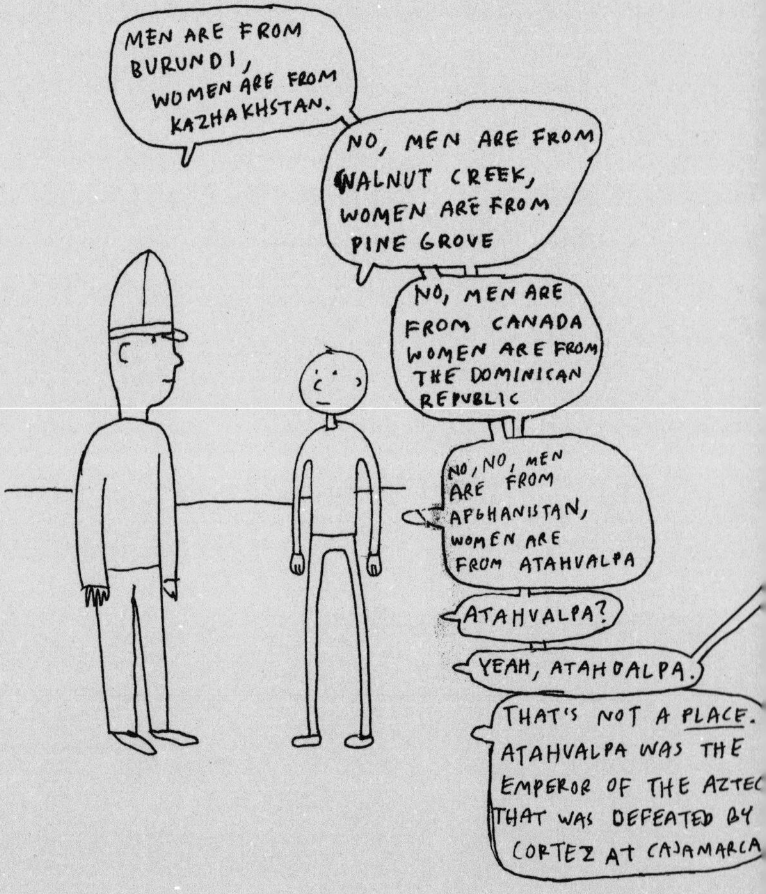
MEN ARE FROM BURUNDI, WOMEN ARE FROM KAZHAKHSTAN.
NO, MEN ARE FROM WALNUT CREEK, WOMEN ARE FROM PINE GROVE
NO, MEN ARE FROM CANADA WOMEN ARE FROM THE DOMINICAN REPUBLIC
NO, NO, MEN ARE FROM AFGHANISTAN, WOMEN ARE FROM ATAHVALPA
ATAHVALPA?
YEAH, ATAHUALPA.
THAT'S NOT A PLACE. ATAHVALPA WAS THE EMPEROR OF THE AZTEC THAT WAS DEFEATED BY CORTEZ AT CAJAMARCA

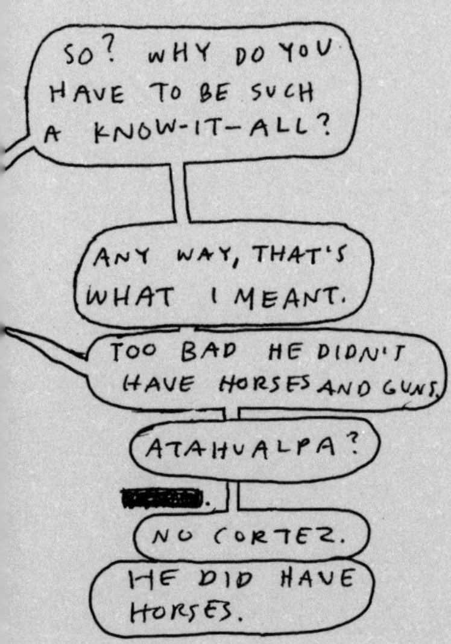
SO? WHY DO YOU HAVE TO BE SUCH A KNOW-IT-ALL?
ANY WAY, THAT'S WHAT I MEANT.
TOO BAD HE DIDN'T HAVE HORSES AND GUNS.
ATAHUALPA?
[redacted].
NO CORTEZ.
HE DID HAVE HORSES.

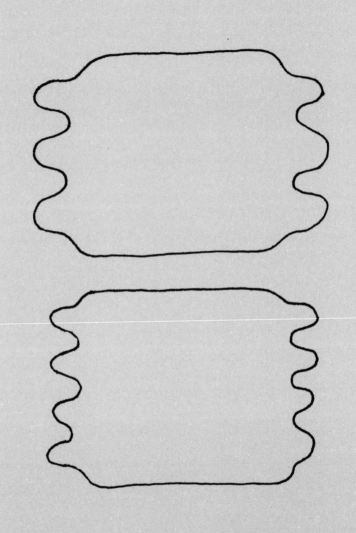

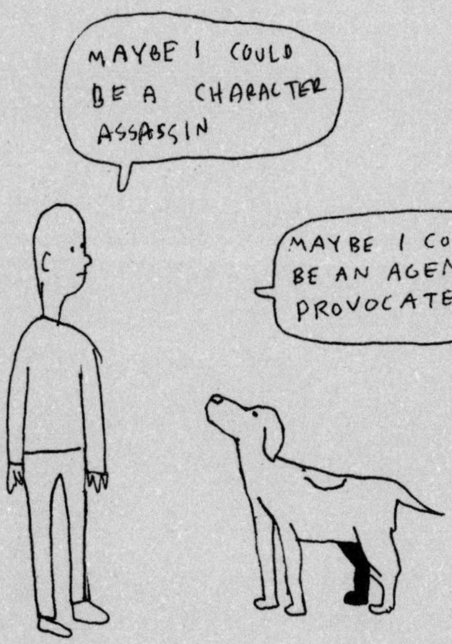
MAYBE I COULD BE A CHARACTER ASSASSIN
MAYBE I COULD BE AN AGENT PROVOCATEUR

job hunt

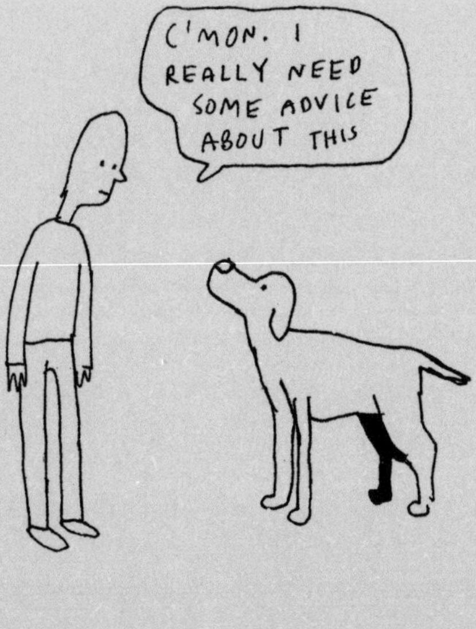
C'MON. I REALLY NEED SOME ADVICE ABOUT THIS

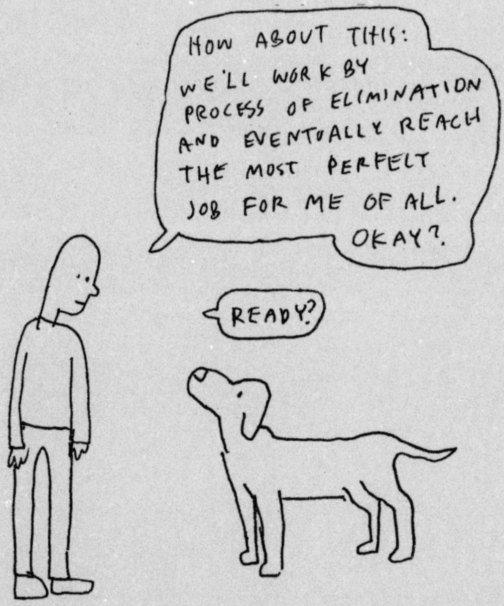
HOW ABOUT THIS: WE'LL WORK BY PROCESS OF ELIMINATION AND EVENTUALLY REACH THE MOST PERFECT JOB FOR ME OF ALL. OKAY?.
READY?

OKAY: CHEMICAL ENGINEER OR BATHROOM ATTENDANT AT A FANCY HOTEL?

YEAH?
OKAY: BATHROOM ATTENDANT AT A FANCY HOTEL OR... LIMOUSINE MECHANIC?
SCRATCH
SCRATCH

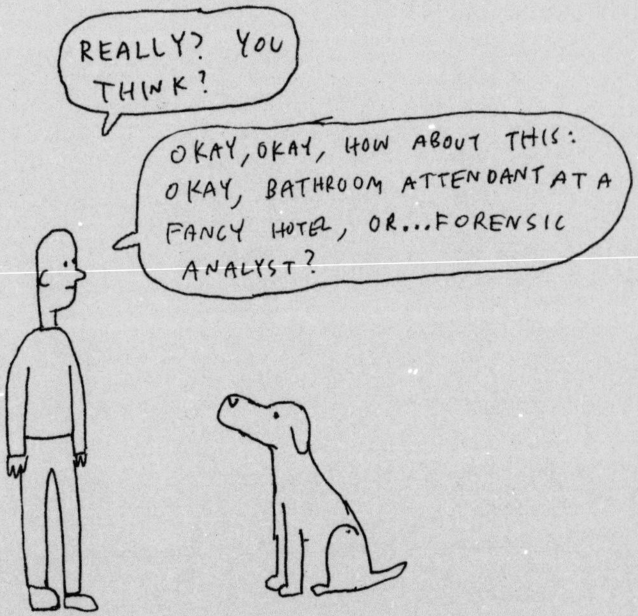
REALLY? YOU THINK?
OKAY, OKAY, HOW ABOUT THIS: OKAY, BATHROOM ATTENDANT AT A FANCY HOTEL, OR...FORENSIC ANALYST?

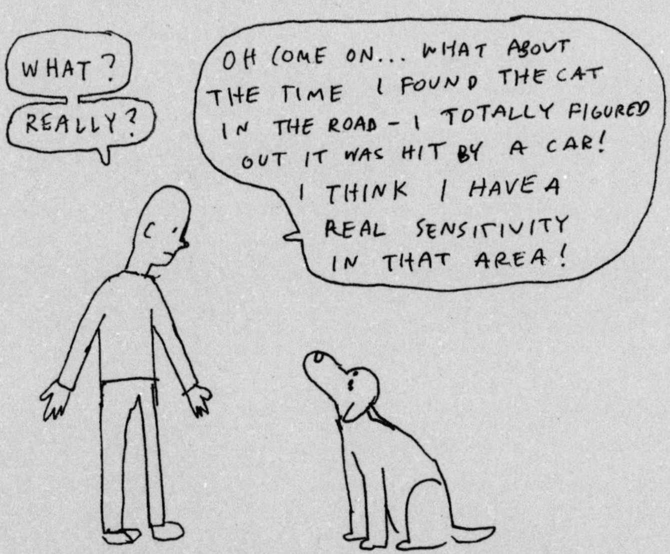
WHAT?
REALLY?
OH COME ON... WHAT ABOUT THE TIME I FOUND THE CAT IN THE ROAD - I TOTALLY FIGURED OUT IT WAS HIT BY A CAR! I THINK I HAVE A REAL SENSITIVITY IN THAT AREA!

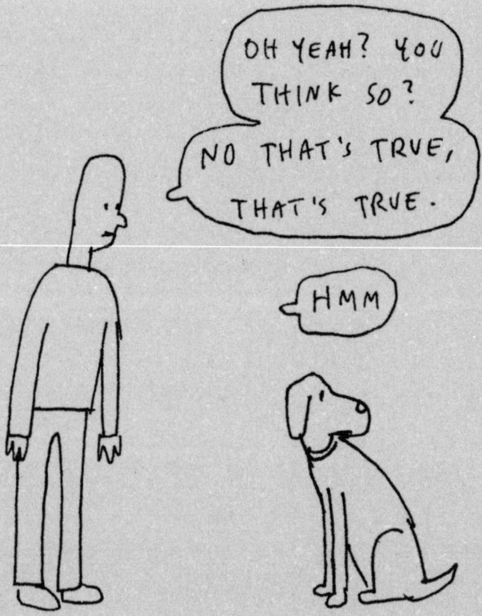
OH YEAH? YOU THINK SO?
NO THAT'S TRUE, THAT'S TRUE.
HMM

SNIFF

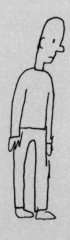

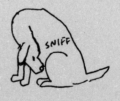

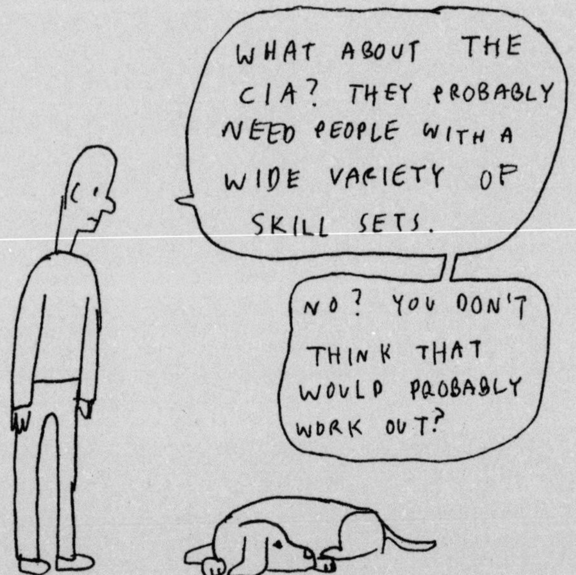
WHAT ABOUT THE CIA? THEY PROBABLY NEED PEOPLE WITH A WIDE VARIETY OF SKILL SETS.
NO? YOU DON'T THINK THAT WOULD PROBABLY WORK OUT?

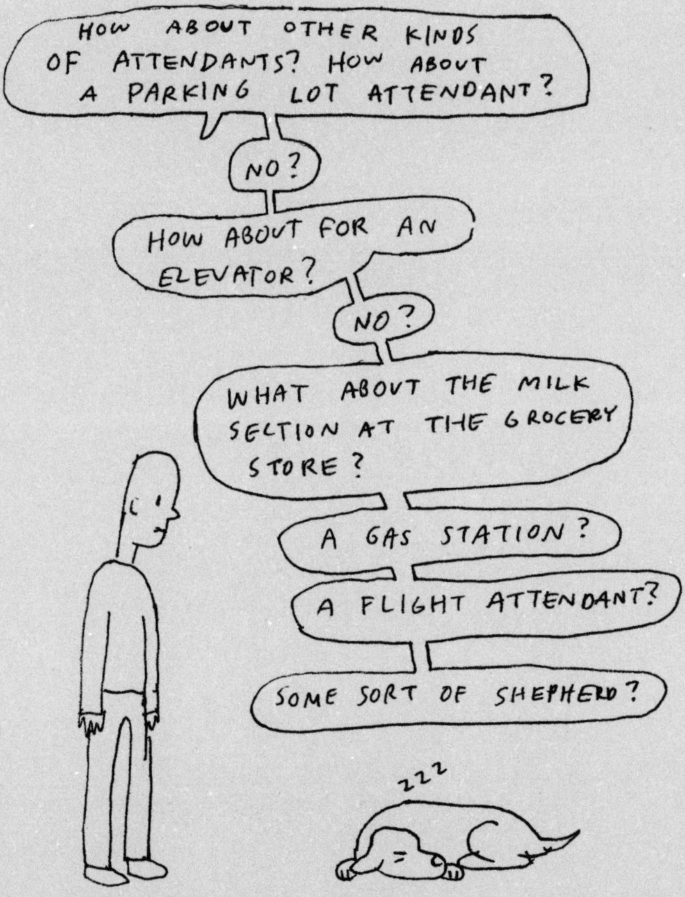
HOW ABOUT OTHER KINDS OF ATTENDANTS? HOW ABOUT A PARKING LOT ATTENDANT?
NO?
HOW ABOUT FOR AN ELEVATOR?
NO?
WHAT ABOUT THE MILK SECTION AT THE GROCERY STORE?
A GAS STATION?
A FLIGHT ATTENDANT?
SOME SORT OF SHEPHERD?
zzz

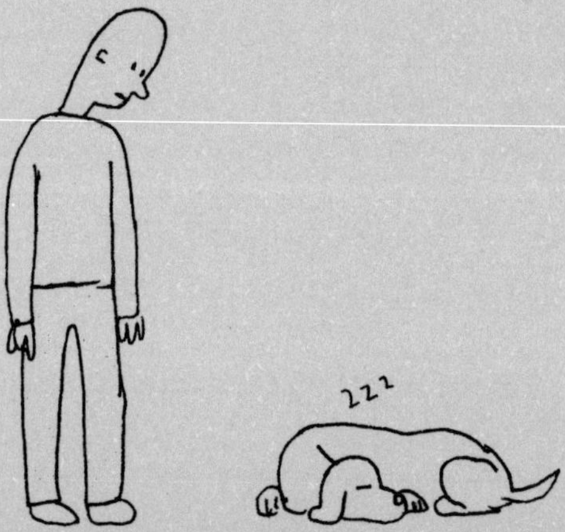
zzz

zzz

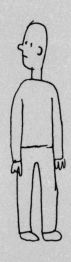

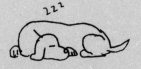

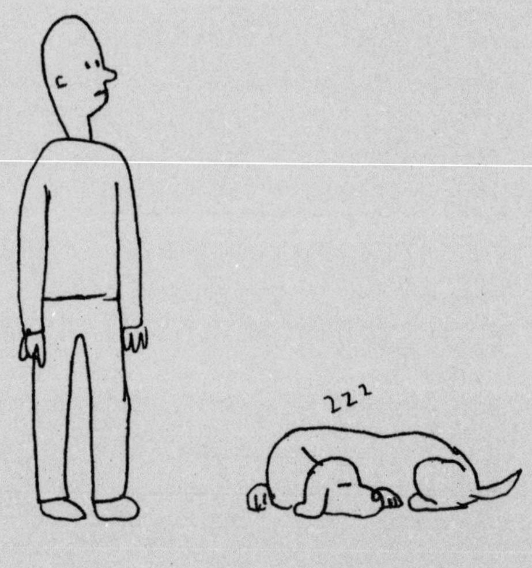
zzz

ALL RIGHT. LET'S TALK ABOUT HOTELS.

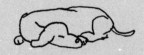

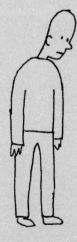

epilogue

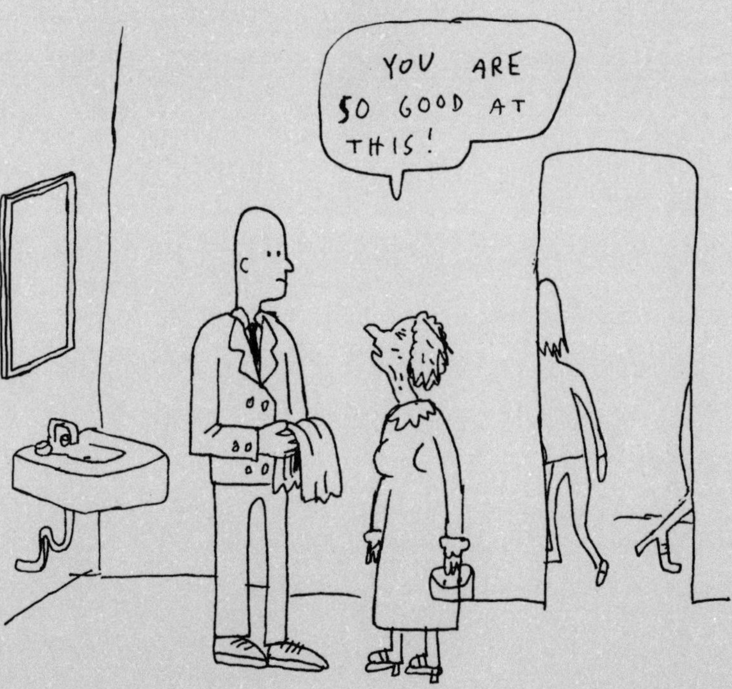
YOU ARE SO GOOD AT THIS!

the wilderness

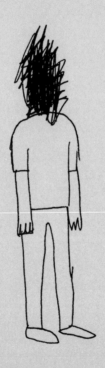

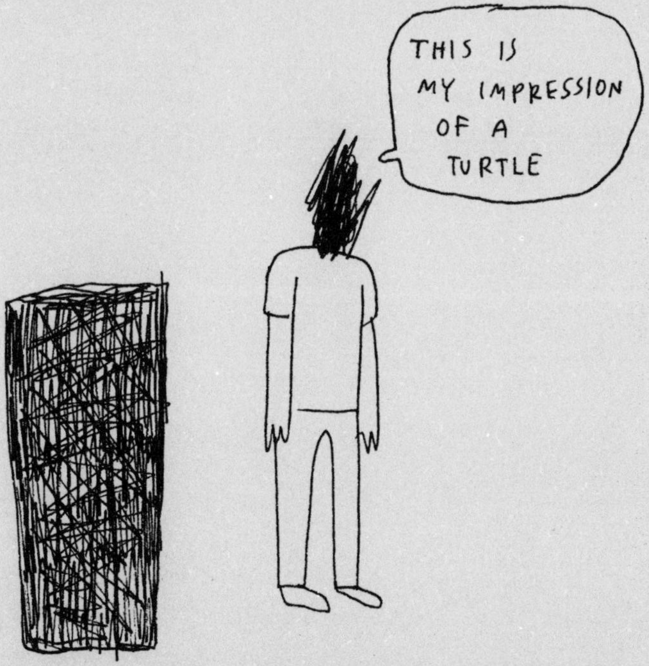
THIS IS MY IMPRESSION OF A TURTLE

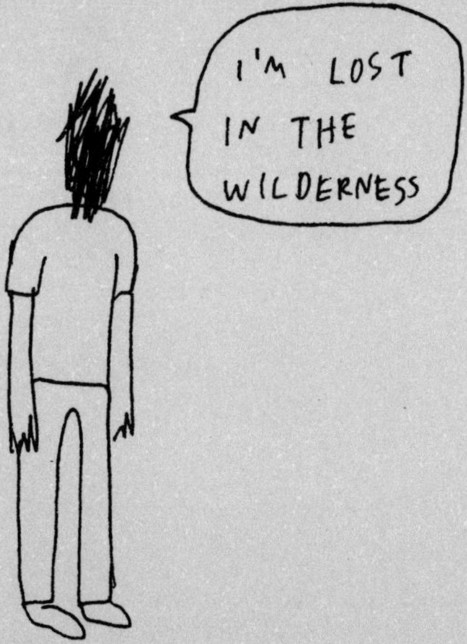
I'M LOST IN THE WILDERNESS

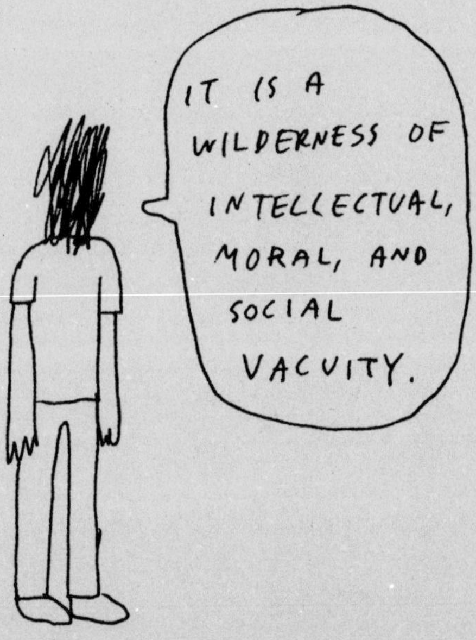
IT IS A WILDERNESS OF INTELLECTUAL, MORAL, AND SOCIAL VACUITY.

EVERYTHING IS BROKEN. NOTHING WORKS.

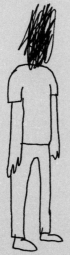

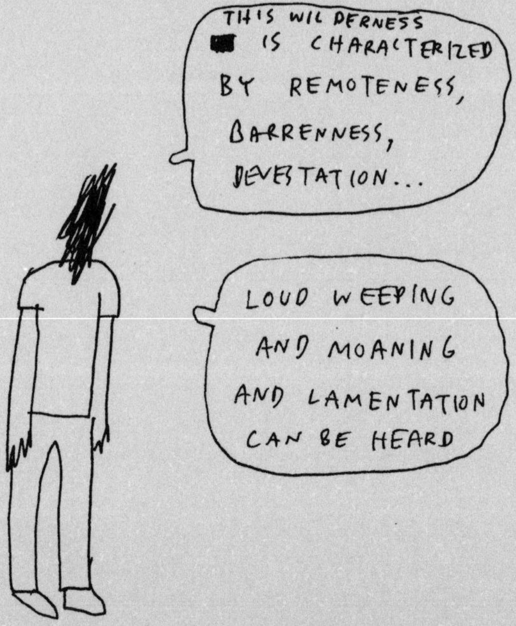
THIS WILDERNESS [redacted] IS CHARACTERIZED BY REMOTENESS, BARRENNESS, DEVESTATION...
LOUD WEEPING AND MOANING AND LAMENTATION CAN BE HEARD

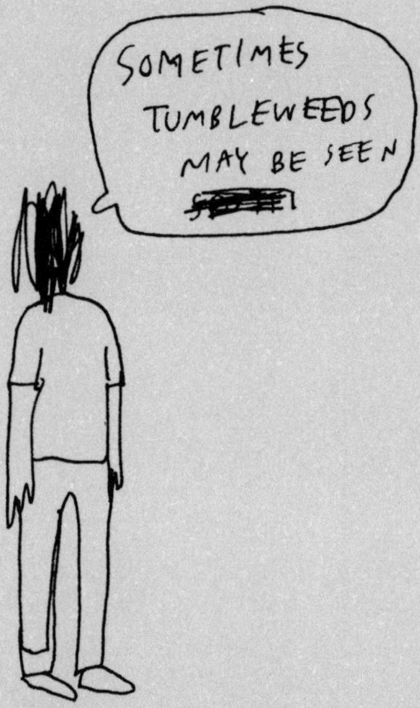
SOMETIMES
TUMBLEWEEDS
MAY BE SEEN

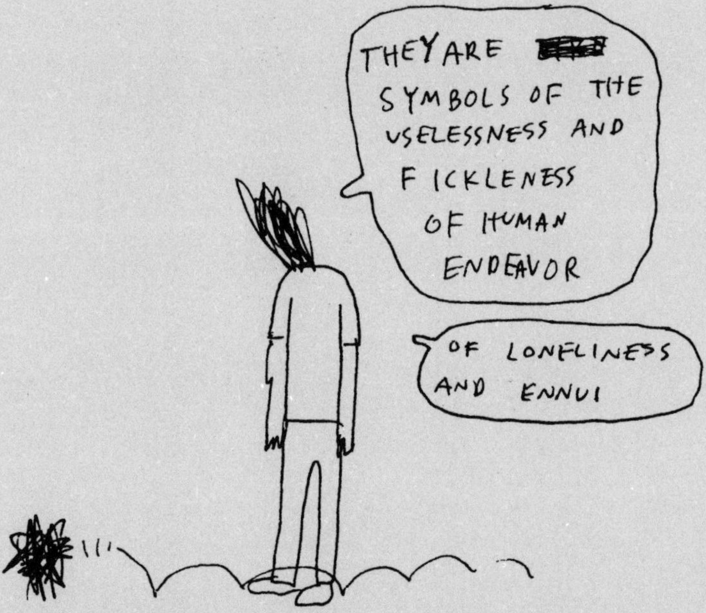
THEY ARE [redacted] SYMBOLS OF THE USELESSNESS AND FICKLENESS OF HUMAN ENDEAVOR
OF LONELINESS AND ENNUI

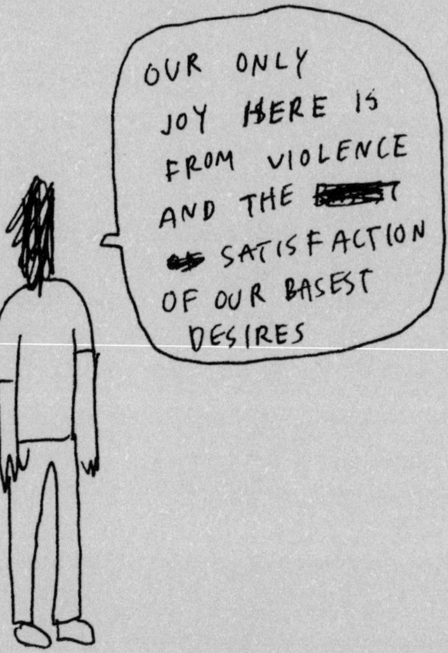
OUR ONLY JOY HERE IS FROM VIOLENCE AND THE SATISFACTION OF OUR BASEST DESIRES

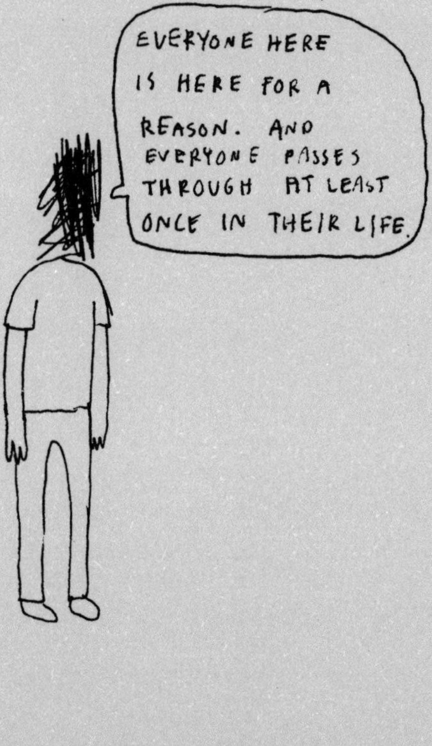
EVERYONE HERE IS HERE FOR A REASON. AND EVERYONE PASSES THROUGH AT LEAST ONCE IN THEIR LIFE.

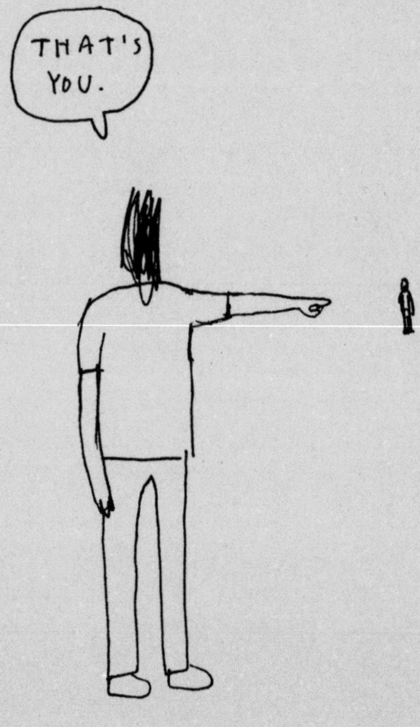
THAT'S YOU.

SOME PEOPLE
ARE HERE FOR ONLY A
FEW MINUTES. OTHERS FOR
YEARS. SOME PEOPLE NEVER
LEAVE.

I RAN INTO MY
AUNT LAST WEEK. SHE
WAS RIDING A GIANT
TUSKED PIG. HER HEAD WAS
ON FIRE. SHE WAS
WAVING A REVOLVER
AND SHOUTING OBSCENITIES.
SHE'S A DEALMAKER.
APPARENTLY SHE'S
BEEN GIVEN SOME
RESPONSIBILITY FOR
RUNNING THINGS.

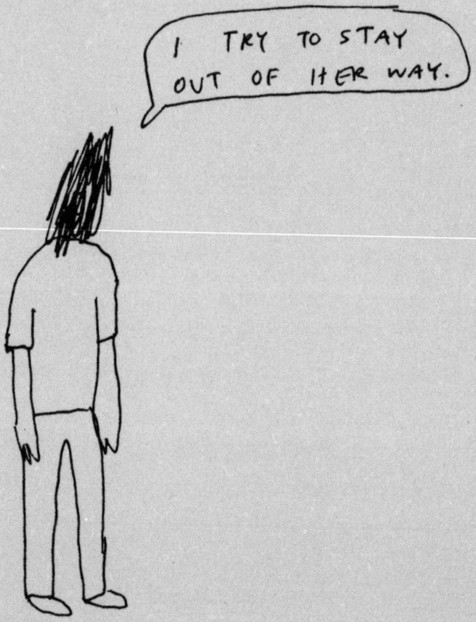
I TRY TO STAY OUT OF HER WAY.

AT NIGHT THE DRY WIND HERE CRACKS YOUR SKIN. IT'S COLD AND BITTER. THE FROST GNAWS LIKE A CANCER. IT'S IMPOSSIBLE TO STOP SHIVERING

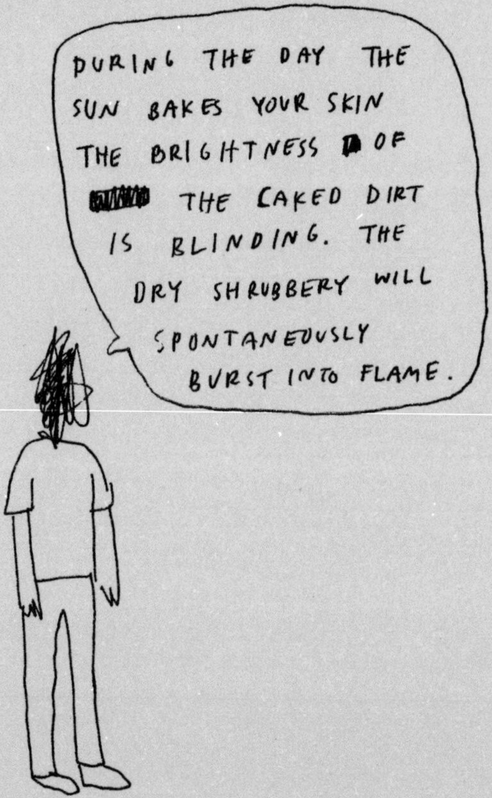

NOTHING EVER HAPPENS HERE, AND YET IMPENDING CATACLYSM IS ALWAYS RIGHT AROUND THE CORNER.

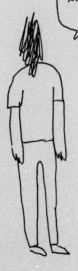

THE ONLY SHOWS ON TV ARE SOAP OPERAS AND GAME SHOWS

ALL RERUNS

AND THE COMMERCIAL BREAKS GO ON FOR DAYS

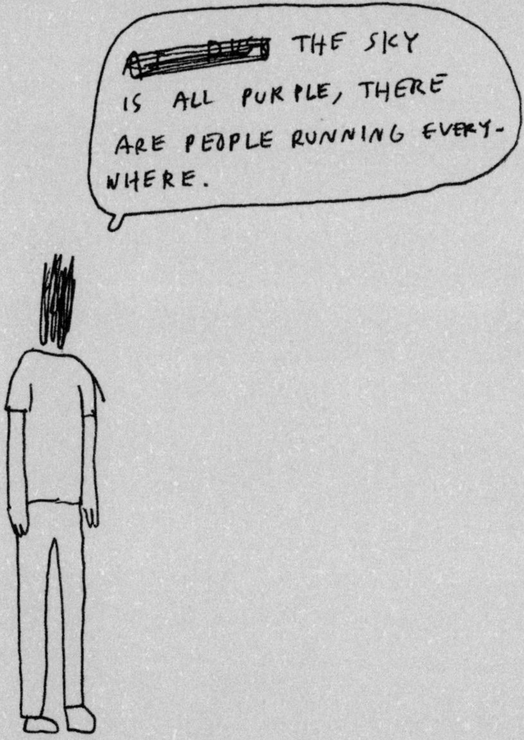
THE SKY IS ALL PURPLE, THERE ARE PEOPLE RUNNING EVERY-WHERE.

DO YOU WANT TO HEAR MORE?
I CAN GO ON...

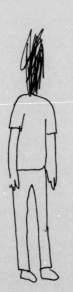

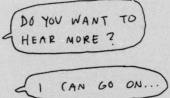

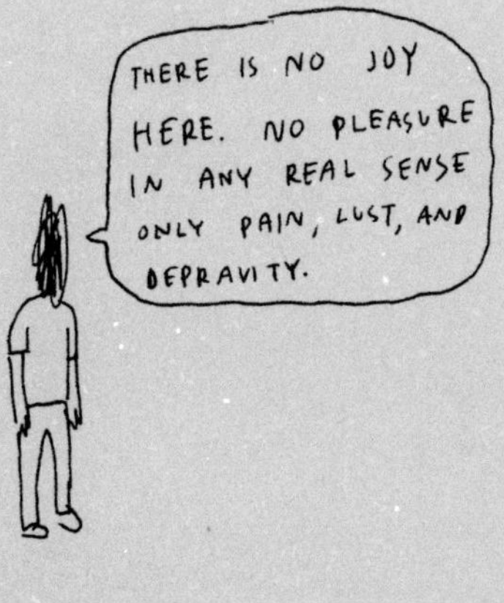
THERE IS NO JOY HERE. NO PLEASURE IN ANY REAL SENSE ONLY PAIN, LUST, AND DEPRAVITY.

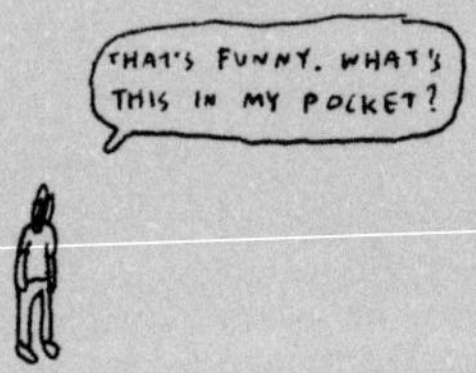
THAT'S FUNNY. WHAT'S THIS IN MY POCKET?

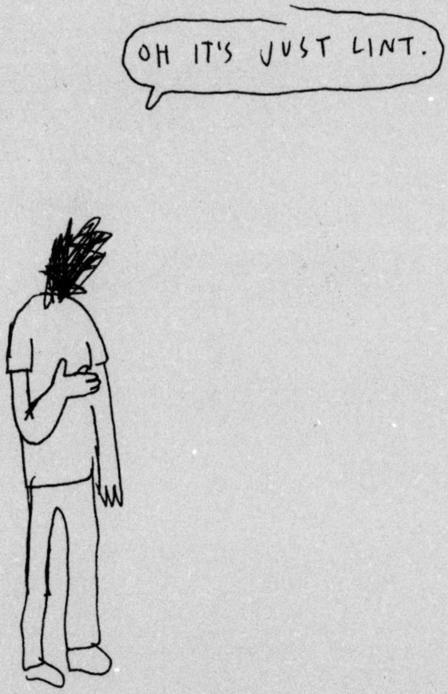
OH IT'S JUST LINT.

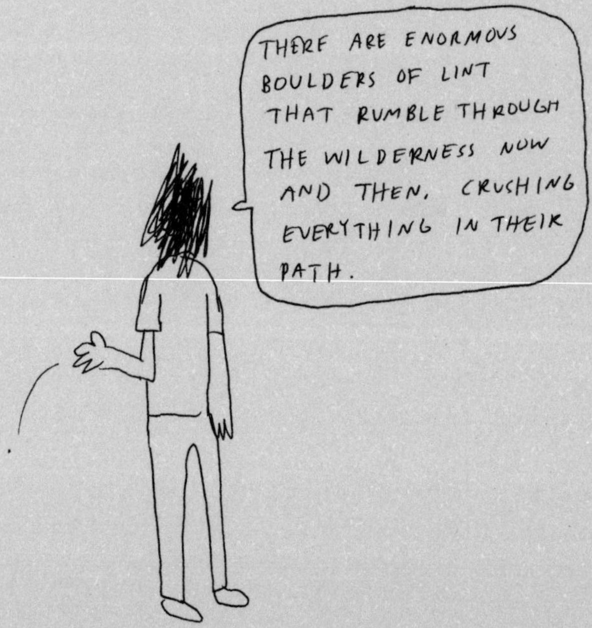
THERE ARE ENORMOUS BOULDERS OF LINT THAT RUMBLE THROUGH THE WILDERNESS NOW AND THEN, CRUSHING EVERYTHING IN THEIR PATH.

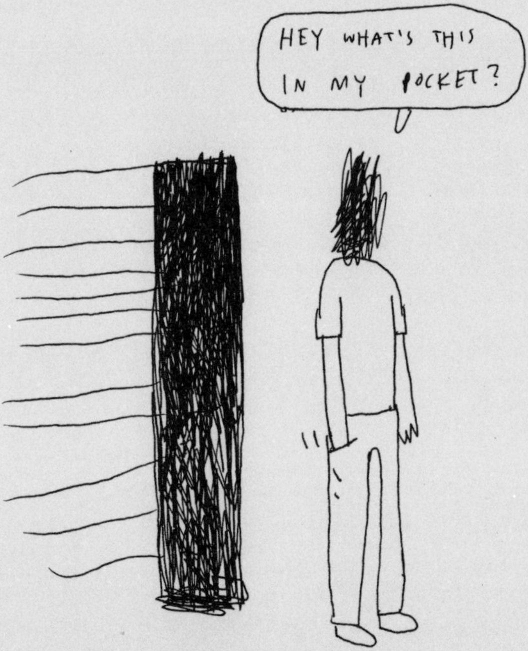
HEY WHAT'S THIS IN MY POCKET?

EVERY DAY ON
THE WALK HOME FROM
SCHOOL, AT THE SAME
PLACE, YOU WOULD FALL

INTO THE DITCH.

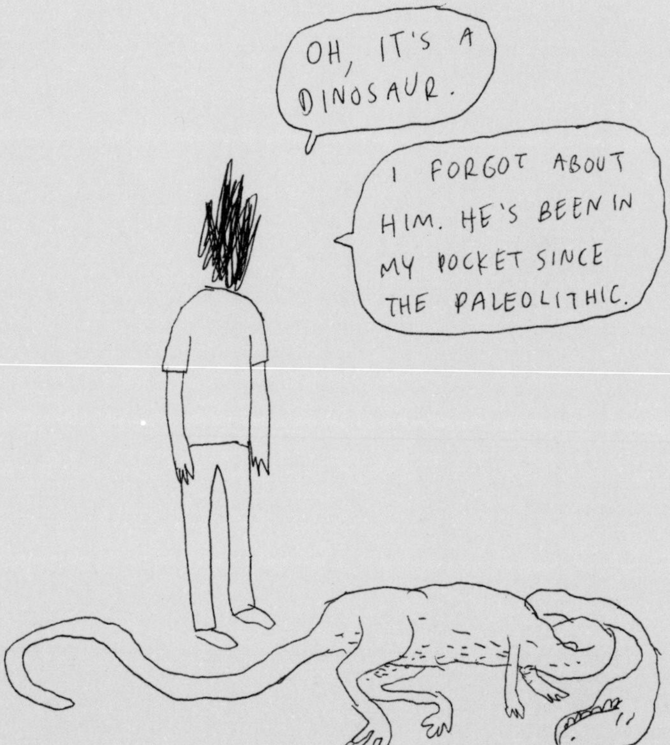
OH, IT'S A DINOSAUR.
I FORGOT ABOUT HIM. HE'S BEEN IN MY POCKET SINCE THE PALEOLITHIC.

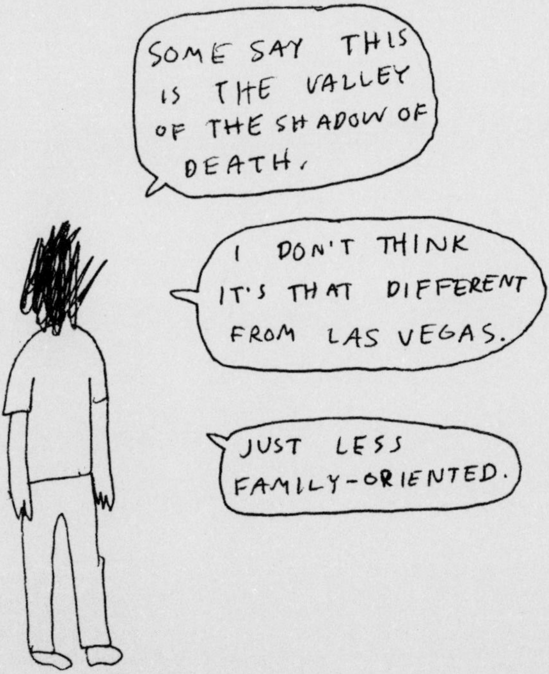
SOME SAY THIS IS THE VALLEY OF THE SHADOW OF DEATH.
I DON'T THINK IT'S THAT DIFFERENT FROM LAS VEGAS.
JUST LESS FAMILY-ORIENTED.

intermission

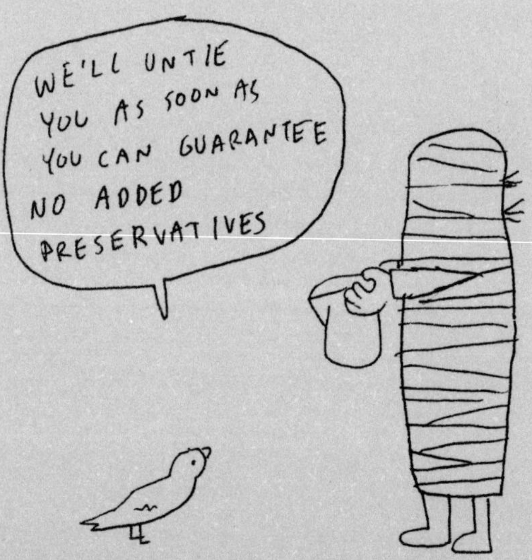
WE'LL UNTIE YOU AS SOON AS YOU CAN GUARANTEE NO ADDED PRESERVATIVES

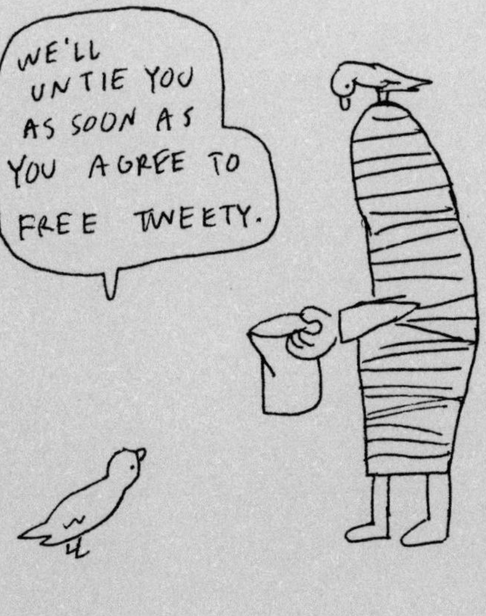
WE'LL UNTIE YOU AS SOON AS YOU AGREE TO FREE TWEETY.

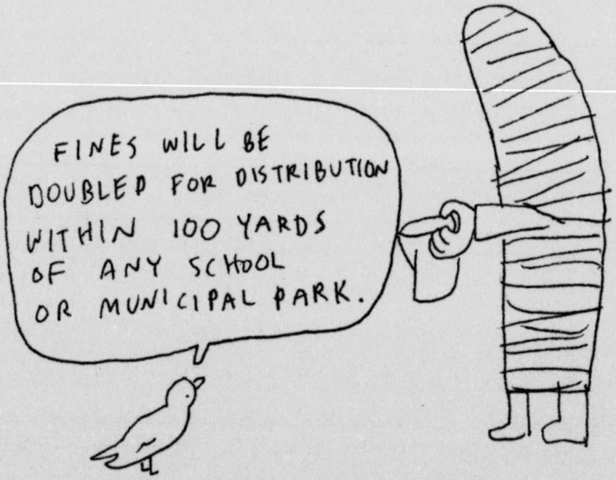
FINES WILL BE DOUBLED FOR DISTRIBUTION WITHIN 100 YARDS OF ANY SCHOOL OR MUNICIPAL PARK.

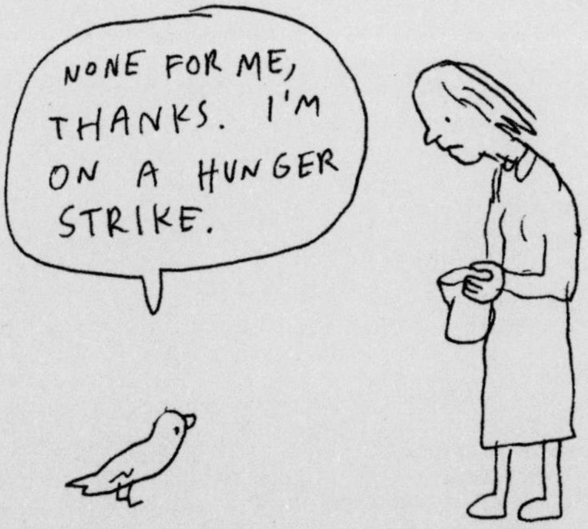
NONE FOR ME, THANKS. I'M ON A HUNGER STRIKE.

DO YOU THINK I'M FAT?

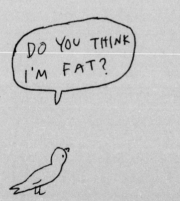

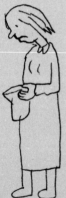

[redacted] [redacted]

[redacted]

[redacted]

[redacted]

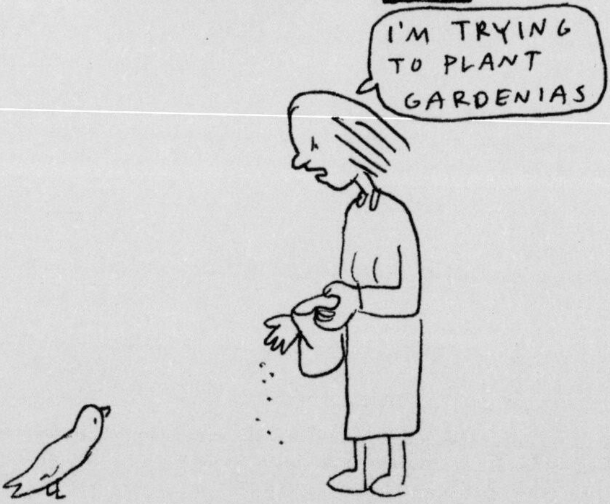
I'M TRYING TO PLANT GARDENIAS

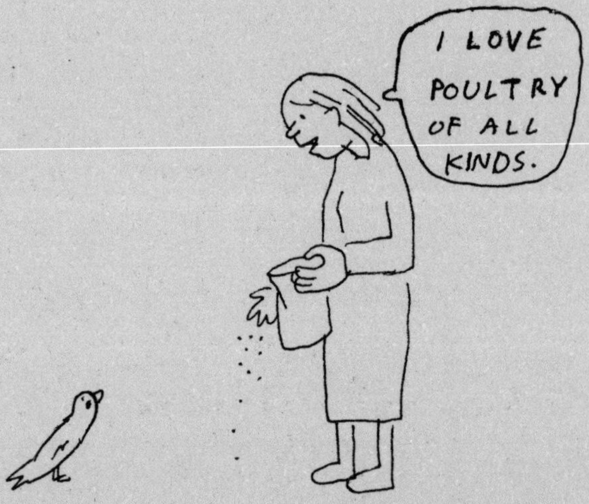
I LOVE POULTRY OF ALL KINDS.

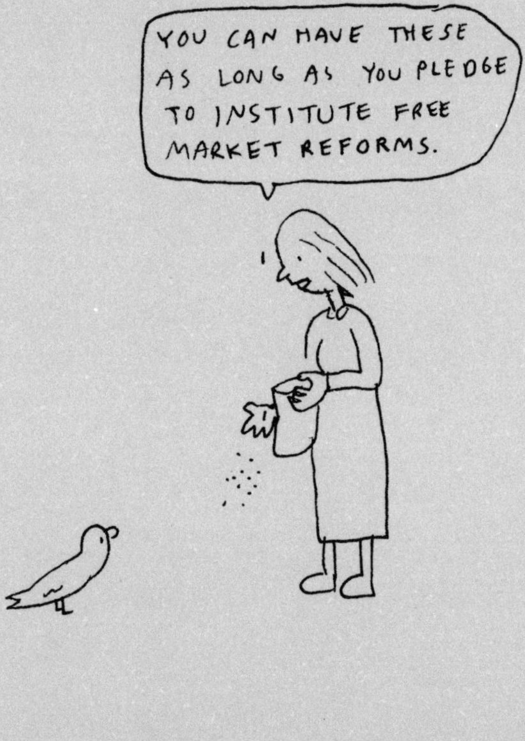
YOU CAN HAVE THESE AS LONG AS YOU PLEDGE TO INSTITUTE FREE MARKET REFORMS.

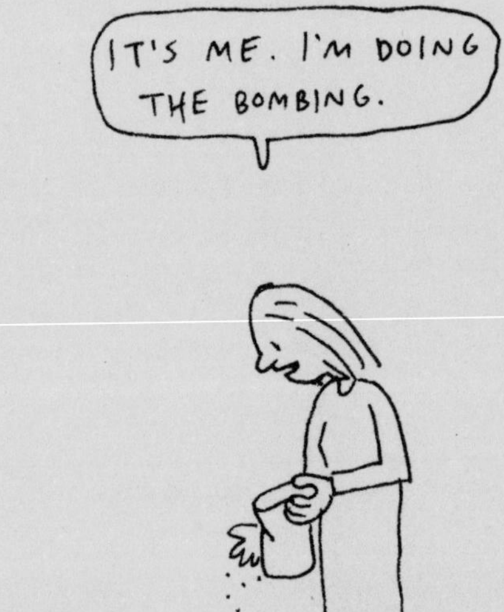
IT'S ME. I'M DOING THE BOMBING.

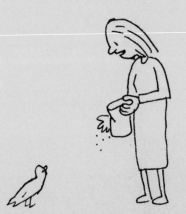

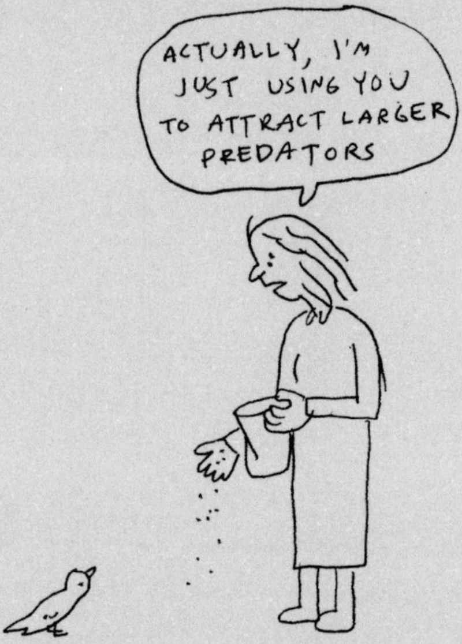
ACTUALLY, I'M JUST USING YOU TO ATTRACT LARGER PREDATORS

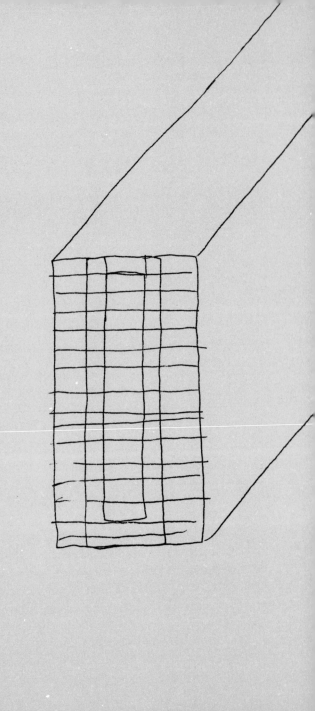

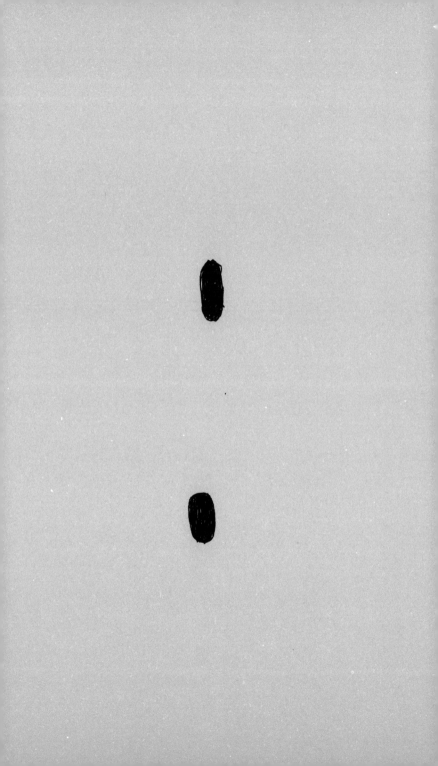

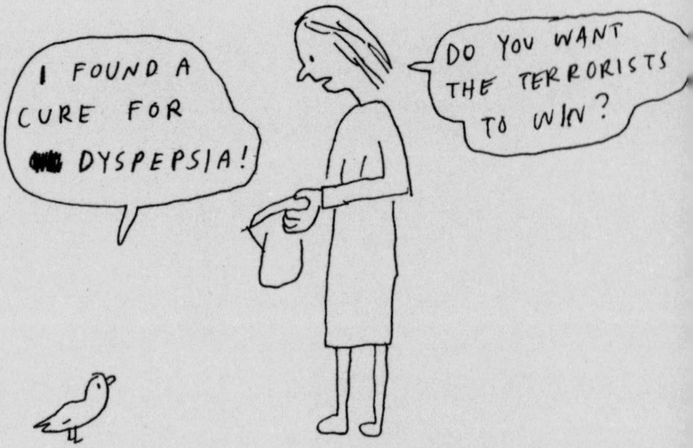

I FOUND A CURE FOR [redacted] DYSPEPSIA!
DO YOU WANT THE TERRORISTS TO WIN?

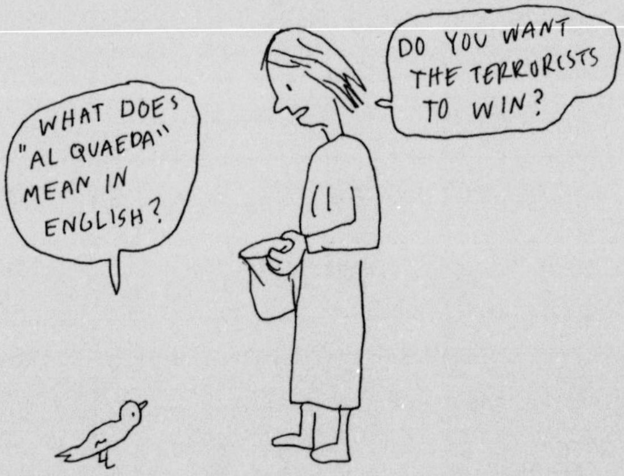

WHAT DOES "AL QUAEDA" MEAN IN ENGLISH?
DO YOU WANT THE TERRORISTS TO WIN?

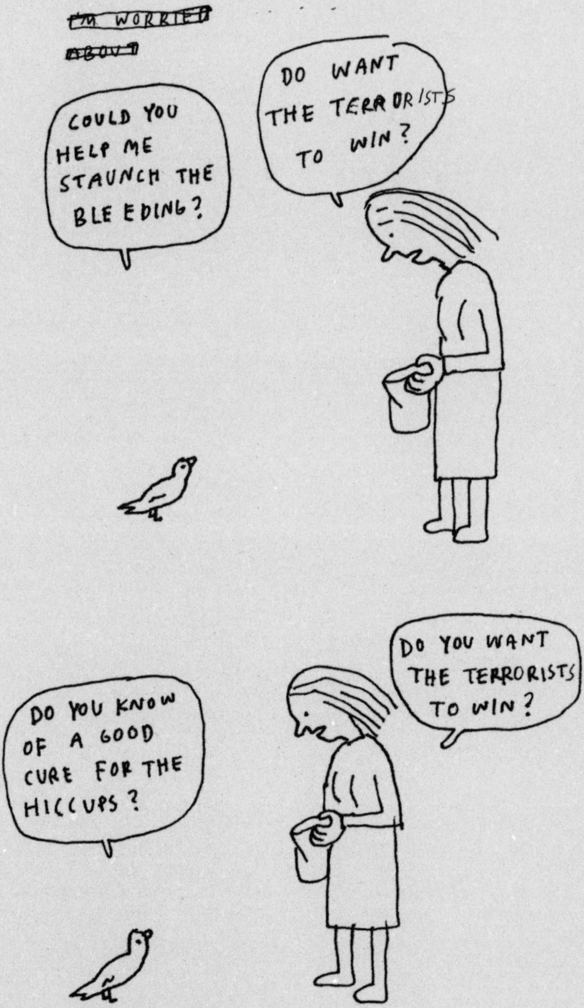
~~I'M WORRIED~~
~~ABOUT~~
COULD YOU HELP ME STAUNCH THE BLEEDING?
DO WANT THE TERRORISTS TO WIN?
DO YOU KNOW OF A GOOD CURE FOR THE HICCUPS?
DO YOU WANT THE TERRORISTS TO WIN?

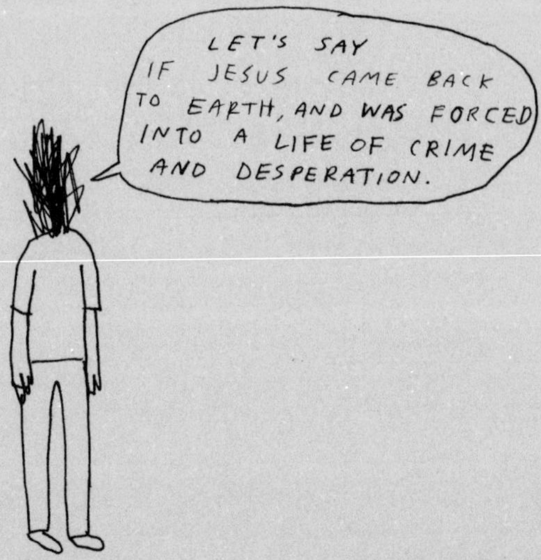
LET'S SAY IF JESUS CAME BACK TO EARTH, AND WAS FORCED INTO A LIFE OF CRIME AND DESPERATION.

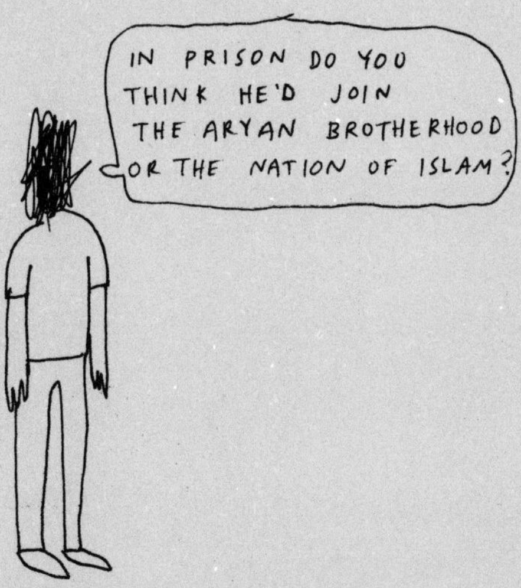
IN PRISON DO YOU THINK HE'D JOIN THE ARYAN BROTHERHOOD OR THE NATION OF ISLAM?

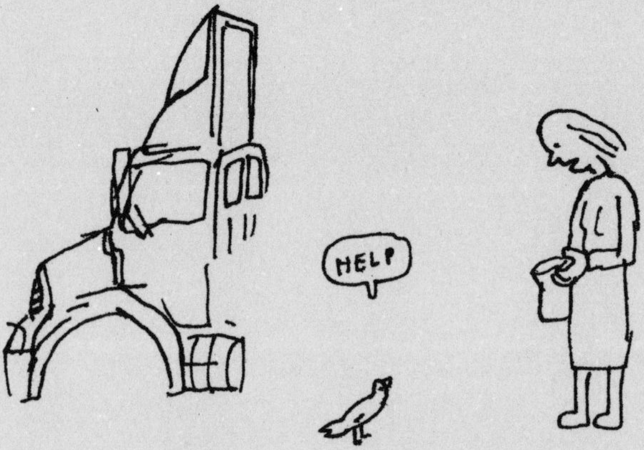
HELP

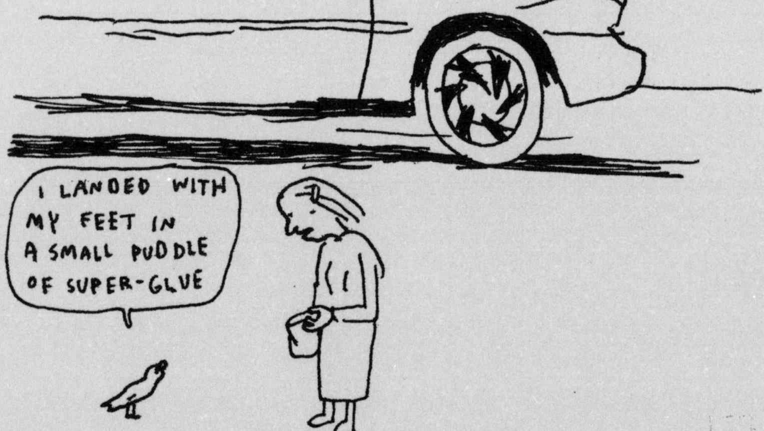
I LANDED WITH MY FEET IN A SMALL PUDDLE OF SUPER-GLUE

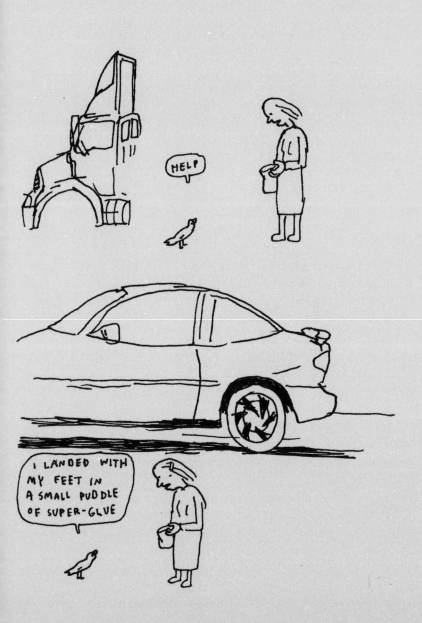

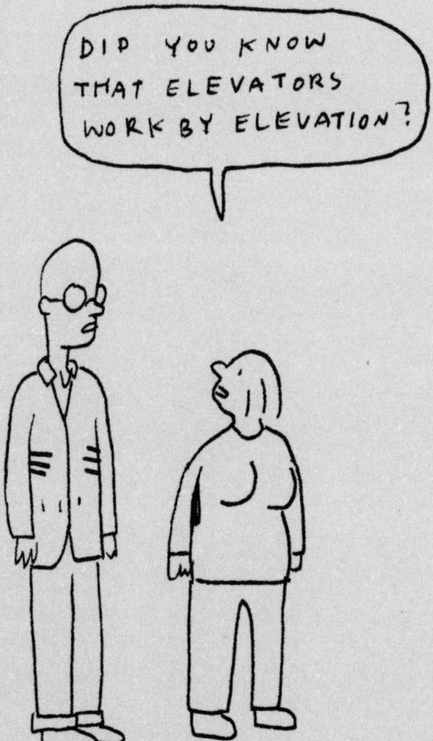
DID YOU KNOW THAT ELEVATORS WORK BY ELEVATION?

IF WE PUT IT ON
ICE ▮▮ ▮ THEY
CAN PROBABLY RE-ATTACH
IT AT THE HOSPITAL

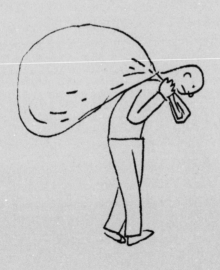

if you meet the buddha
on the road

FIRST NOBLE PRECEPT:
PRE-TREAT HEAVILY SOILED AREAS BY APPLYING NEW TIDE ULTRA DIRECTLY ONTO FABRIC AND RUB.

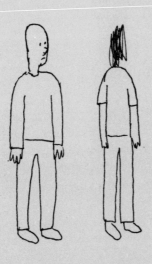

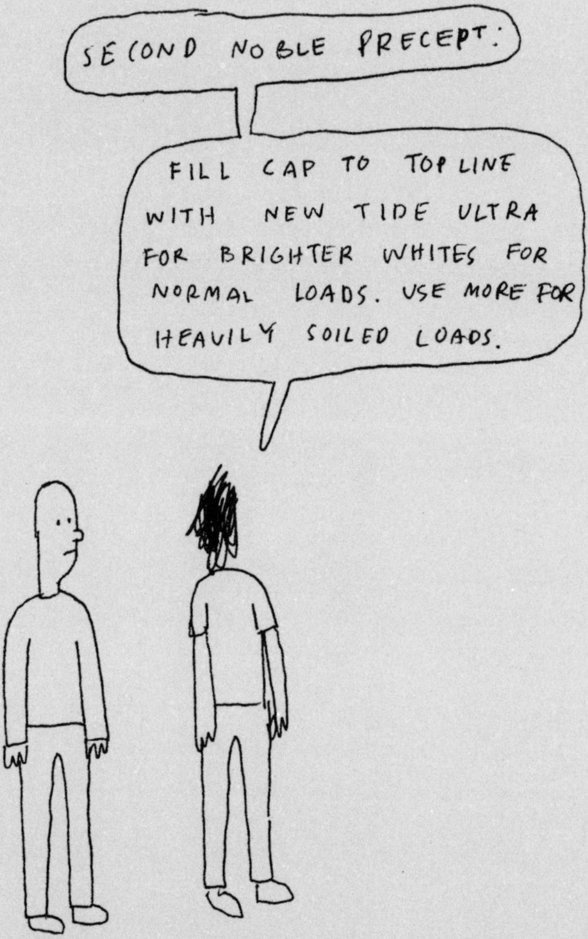
SECOND NOBLE PRECEPT:
FILL CAP TO TOP LINE WITH NEW TIDE ULTRA FOR BRIGHTER WHITES FOR NORMAL LOADS. USE MORE FOR HEAVILY SOILED LOADS.

THIRD NOBLE PRECEPT:
NEW OIL OF OLAY AVOCADO BATH SALTS WILL REDUCE WRINKLING BY 67%.

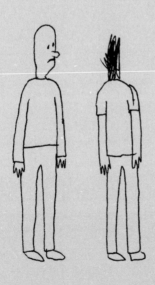

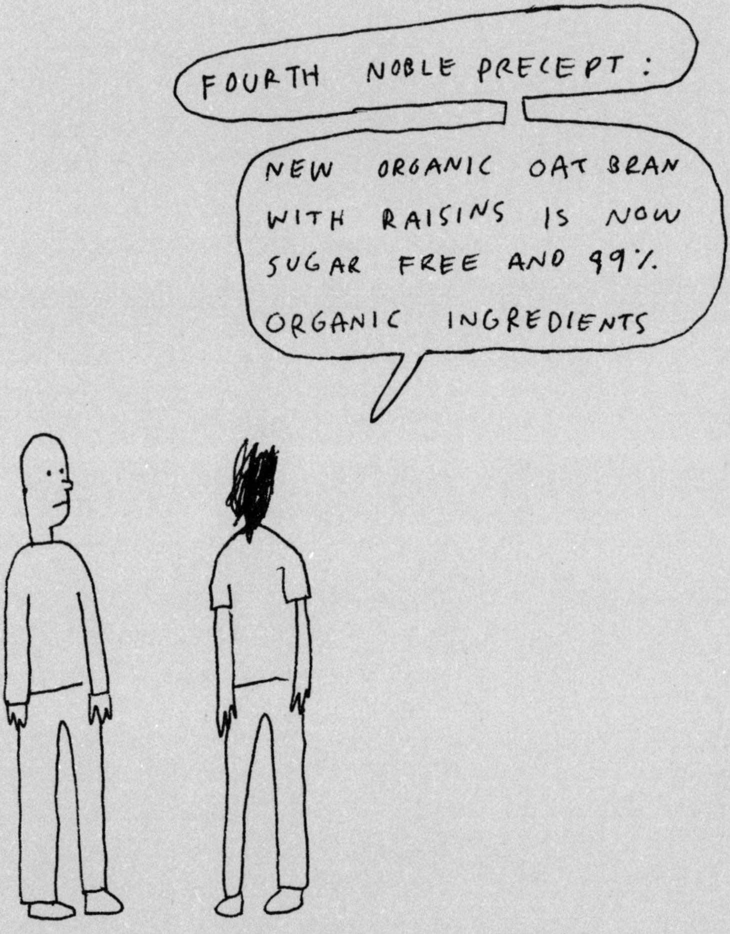
FOURTH NOBLE PRECEPT:
NEW ORGANIC OAT BRAN WITH RAISINS IS NOW SUGAR FREE AND 99% ORGANIC INGREDIENTS

NOW MEDITATE ON THE FOUR NOBLE PRECEPTS AND HOW THEY CAN APPLY TO YOUR LIFE.
IT WILL BRING YOU GREAT PEACE AND CONTENTMENT AND MAKE YOUR ARMS GROW LONGER.
I'LL BE BACK TO QUIZ YOU LATER.

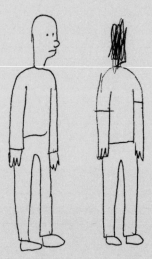

LATER:

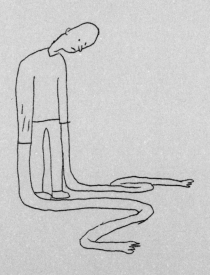

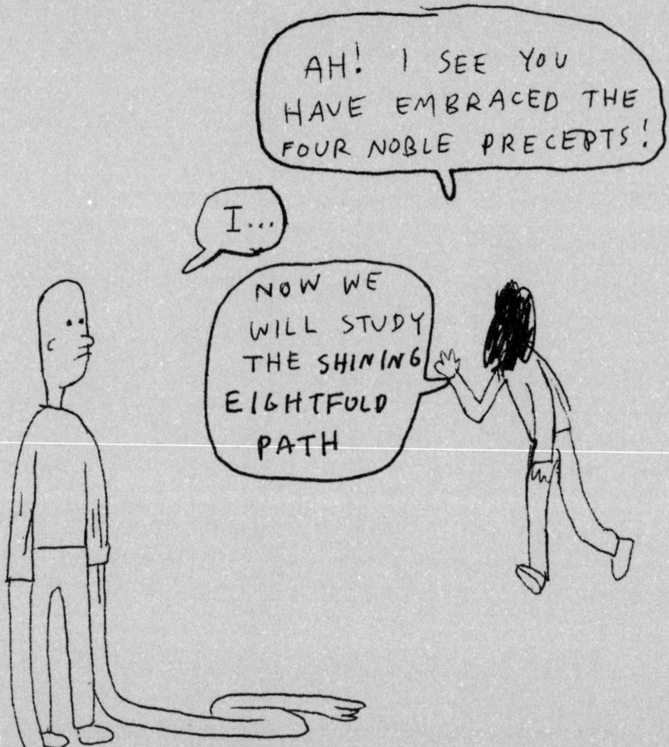
AH! I SEE YOU HAVE EMBRACED THE FOUR NOBLE PRECEPTS!
I...
NOW WE WILL STUDY THE SHINING EIGHTFOLD PATH

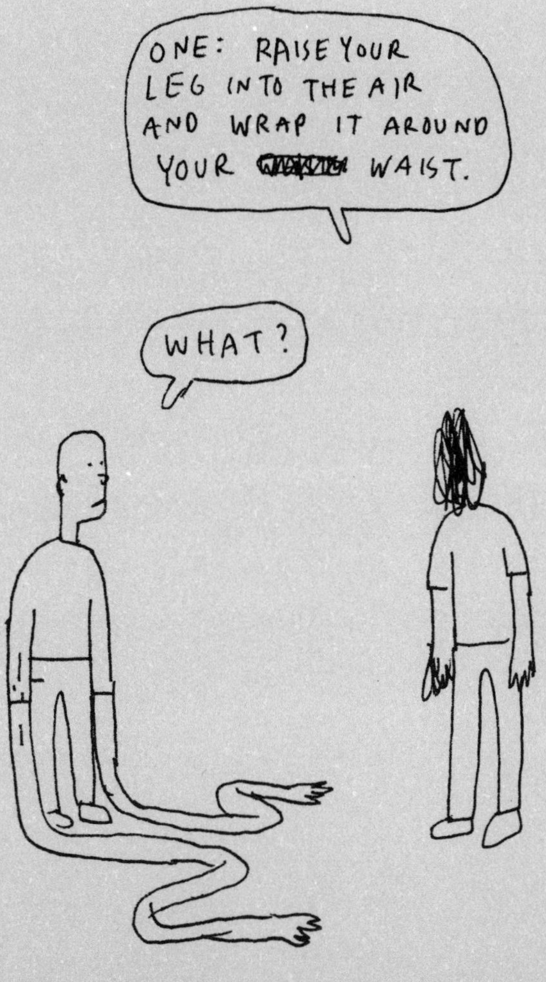
ONE: RAISE YOUR LEG INTO THE AIR AND WRAP IT AROUND YOUR WAIST.
WHAT?

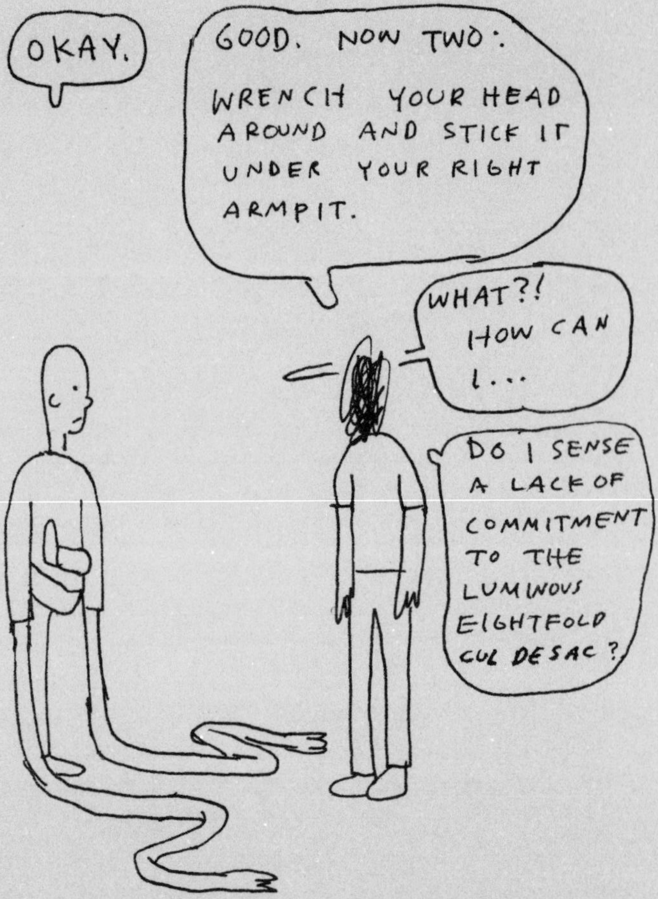
OKAY.
GOOD. NOW TWO: WRENCH YOUR HEAD AROUND AND STICK IT UNDER YOUR RIGHT ARMPIT.
WHAT?! HOW CAN I...
DO I SENSE A LACK OF COMMITMENT TO THE LUMINOUS EIGHTFOLD CUL DE SAC?

GREAT, GREAT. OKAY NOW MEDITATE ON THE RADIANT EIGHTFOLD WATERWAY. I'LL BE BACK IN A WHILE. I HAVE TO MEET SOME FRIENDS TO WATCH THE GAME.
WAIT— BUT THAT'S ONLY TWO— AREN'T THERE SIX MORE?
THAT'S THE GREAT MYSTERY OF THE REDOLENT EIGHTFOLD RIVERWALK.

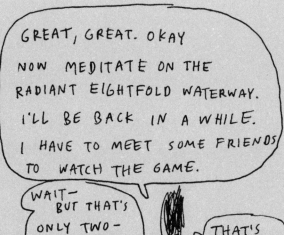

ANY WAY, I'D BE GLAD ABOUT THAT IF I WERE YOU.
NGK
NGK

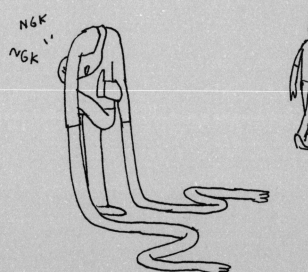

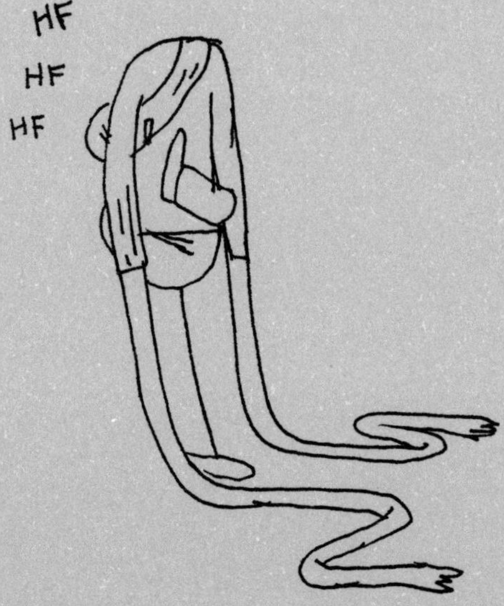
HF
HF
HF

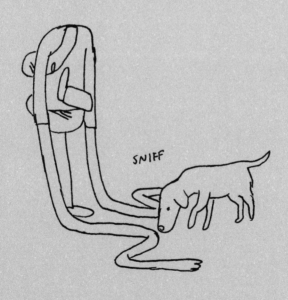

SNIFF

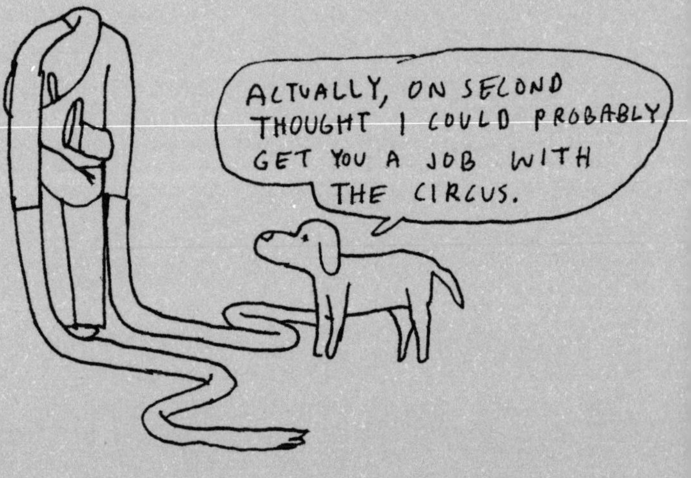
ACTUALLY, ON SECOND THOUGHT I COULD PROBABLY GET YOU A JOB WITH THE CIRCUS.

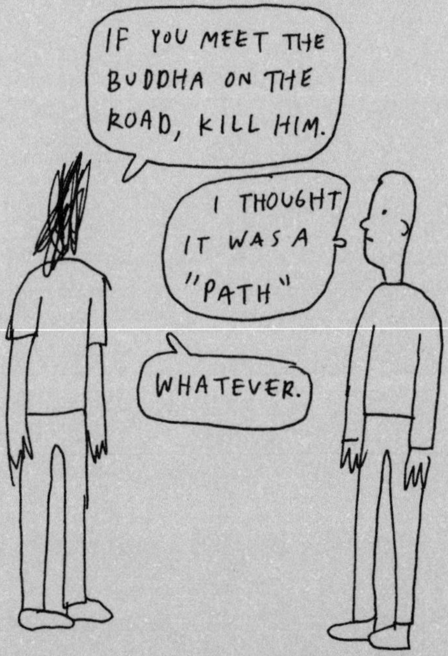
IF YOU MEET THE BUDDHA ON THE ROAD, KILL HIM.
I THOUGHT IT WAS A "PATH"
WHATEVER.

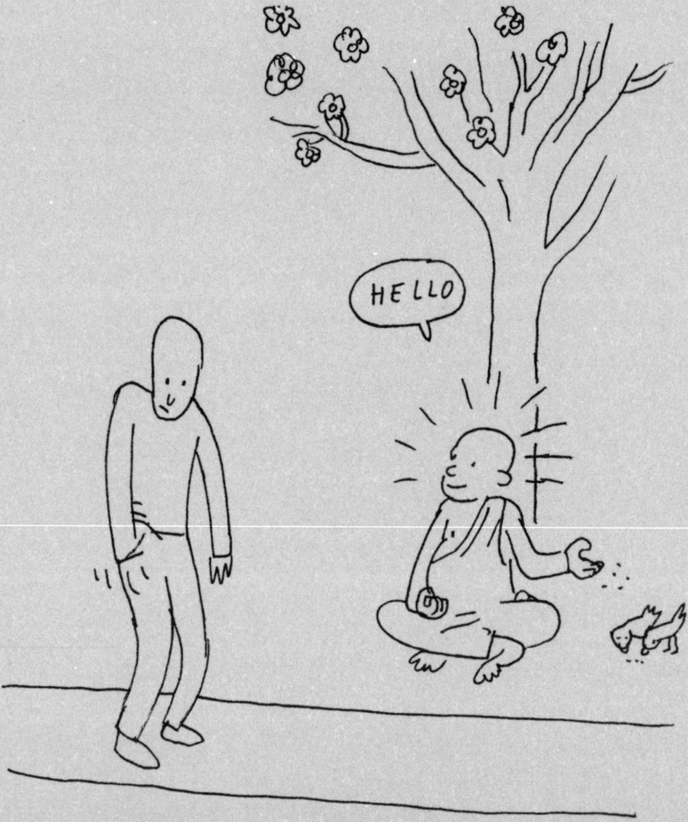
HELLO

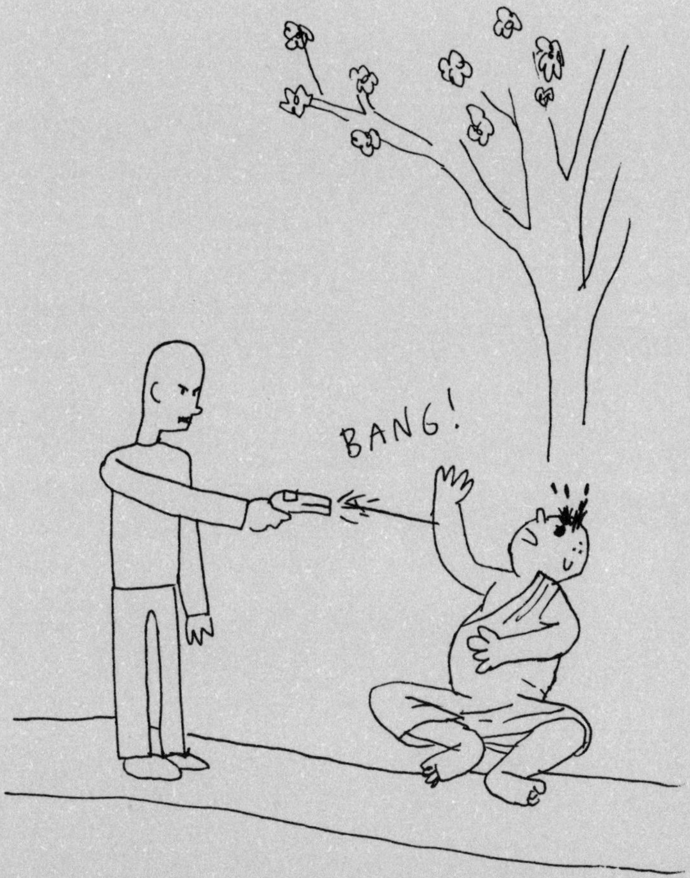
BANG!

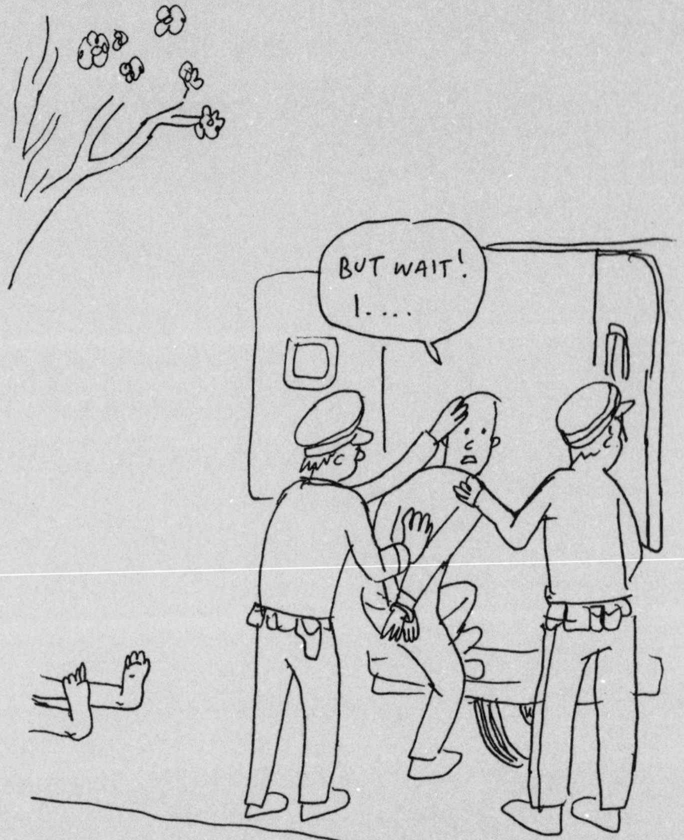
BUT WAIT! I....

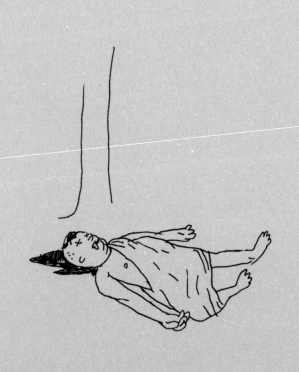

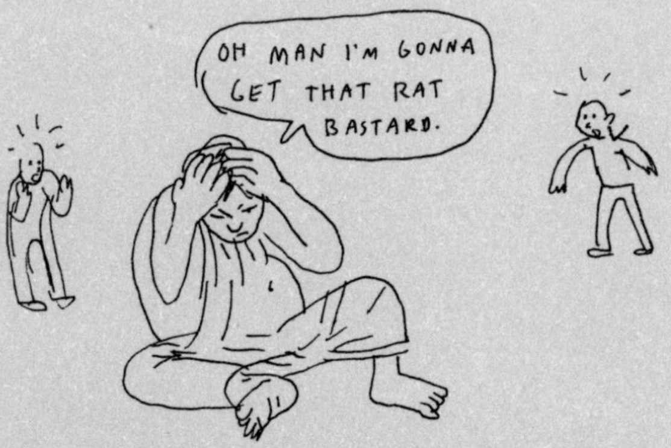
OH MAN I'M GONNA GET THAT RAT BASTARD.

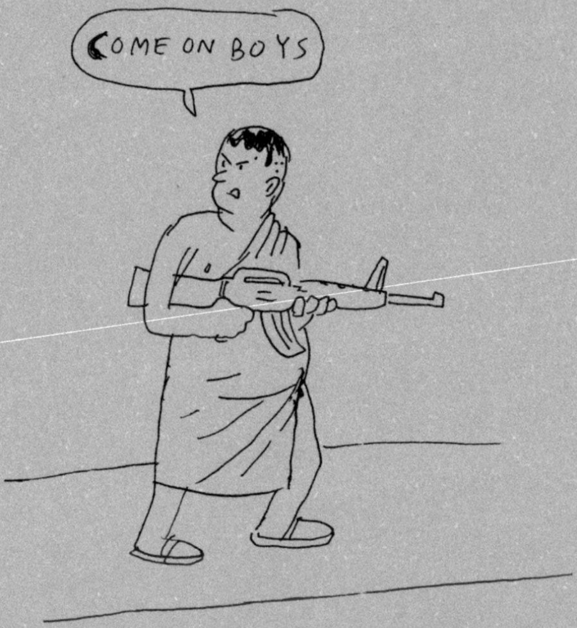
COME ON BOYS

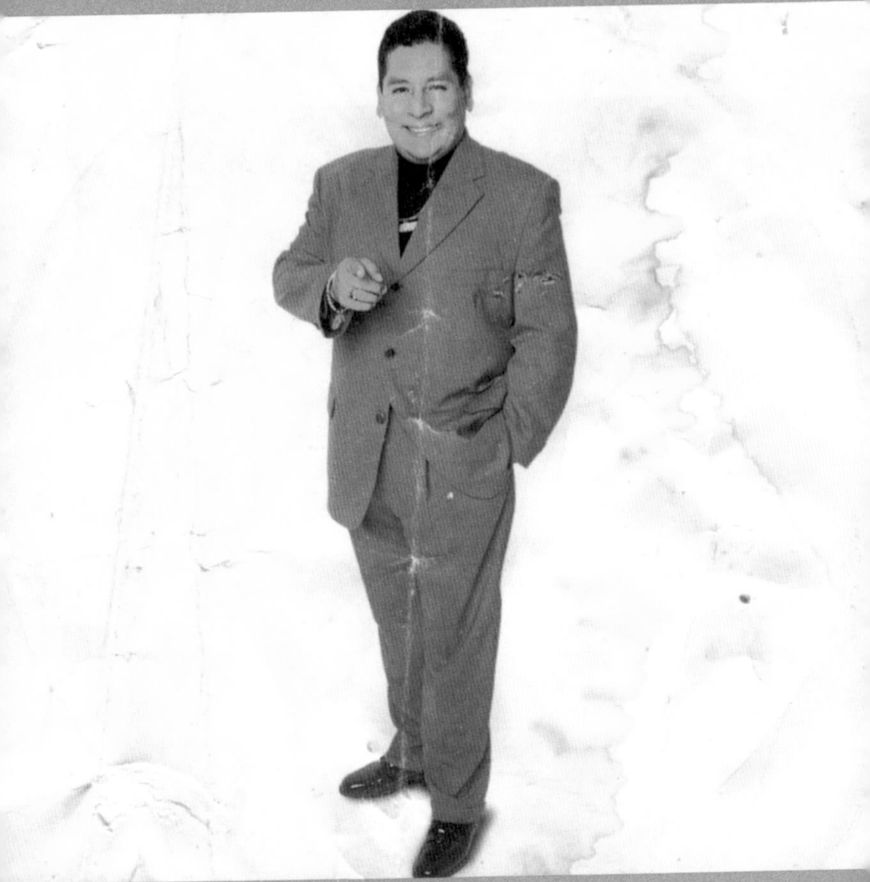

Me volví a acordar de ti • 2. La princesita sueña • 3. Te voy a enamorar • 4. Quinceañera • 5. El prim
amor • 6. Que levante la mano • 7. Está muy sola la niña • 8. El último beso • 9. Mi llamada • 10.

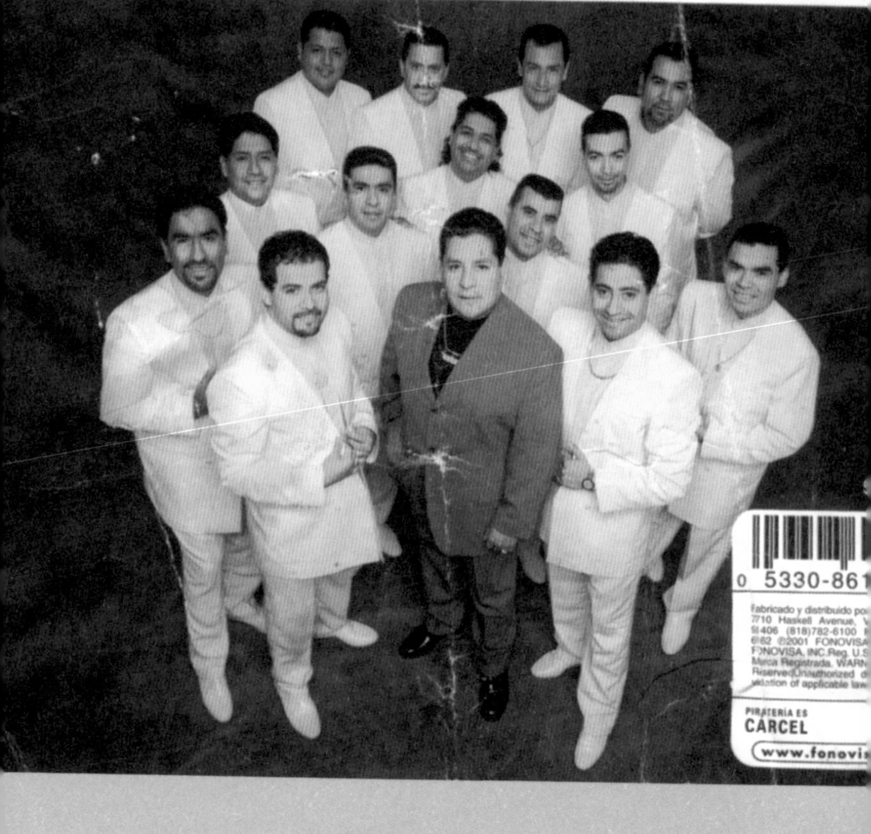
0 5330-861
Fabricado y distribuido po
7710 Haskell Avenue,
91406 (818)782-6100
6162 ©2001 FONOVISA
FONOVISA, INC.Reg. U.S
Marca Registrada. WARN
Reserved.Unauthorized
violation of applicable law
PIRATERÍA ES
CARCEL
www.fonovis

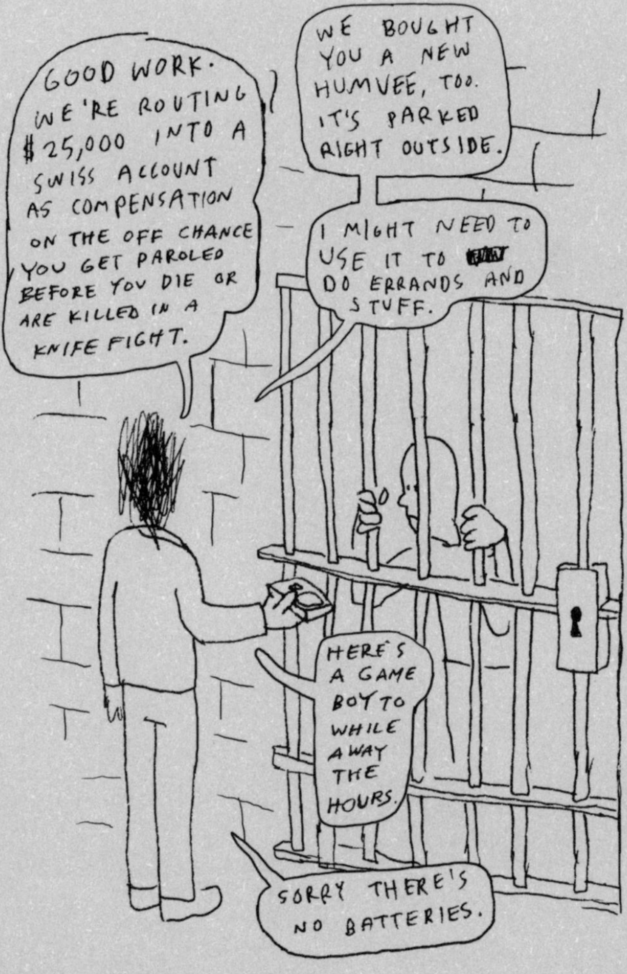
GOOD WORK. WE'RE ROUTING $25,000 INTO A SWISS ACCOUNT AS COMPENSATION ON THE OFF CHANCE YOU GET PAROLED BEFORE YOU DIE OR ARE KILLED IN A KNIFE FIGHT.
WE BOUGHT YOU A NEW HUMVEE, TOO. IT'S PARKED RIGHT OUTSIDE.
I MIGHT NEED TO USE IT TO [redacted] DO ERRANDS AND STUFF.
HERE'S A GAME BOY TO WHILE AWAY THE HOURS.
SORRY THERE'S NO BATTERIES.

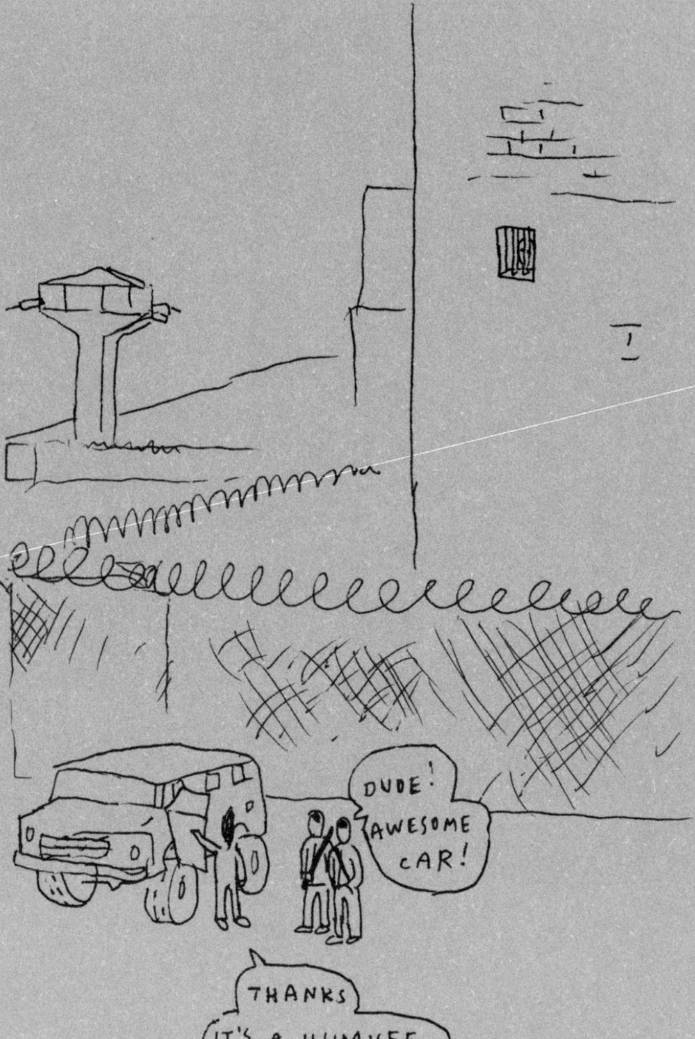
DUDE! AWESOME CAR!
THANKS
IT'S A HUMVEE.

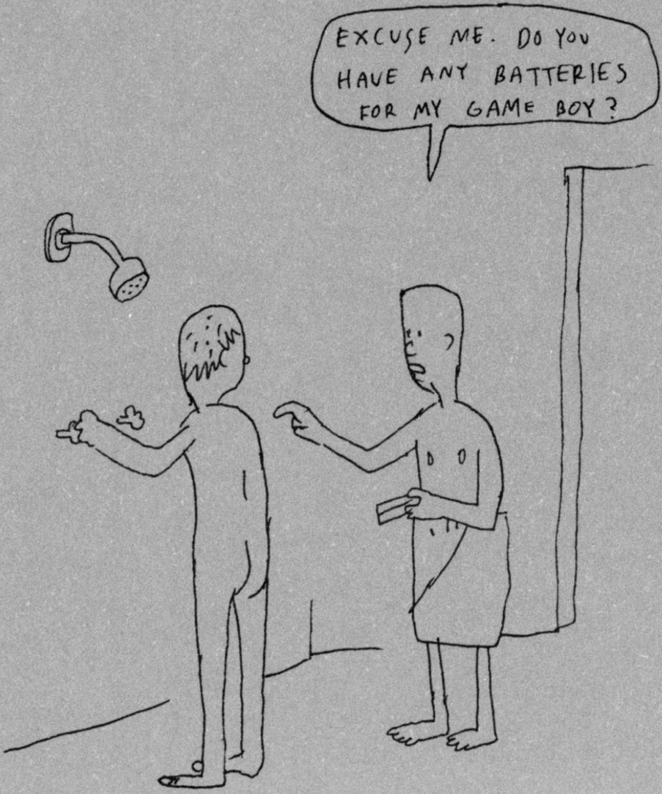
EXCUSE ME. DO YOU HAVE ANY BATTERIES FOR MY GAME BOY?

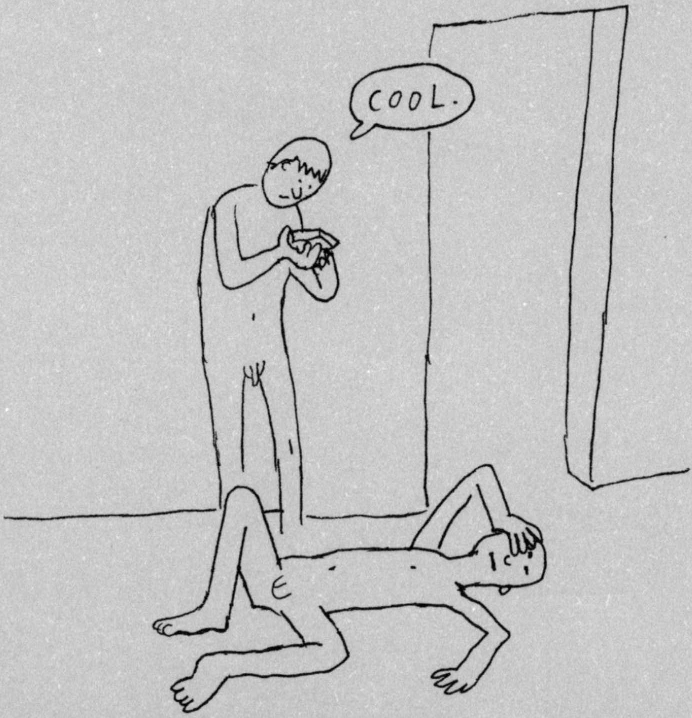
COOL.

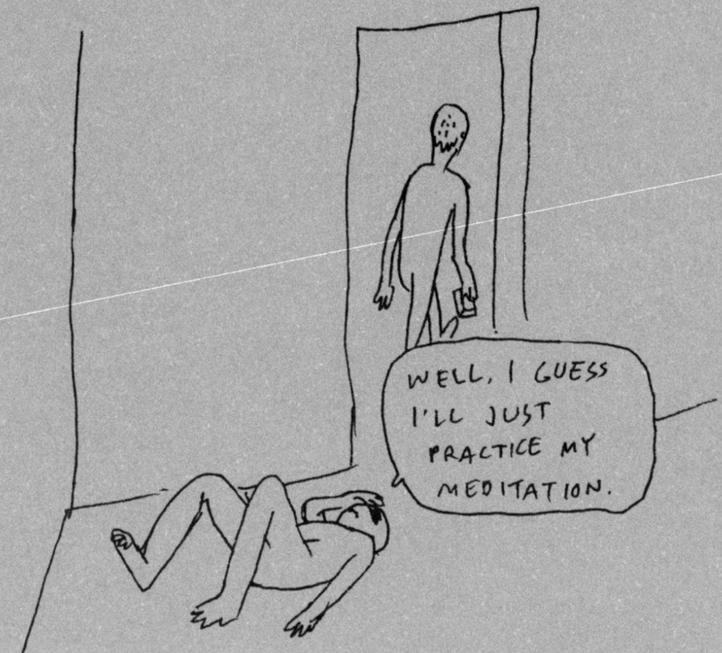
WELL, I GUESS I'LL JUST PRACTICE MY MEDITATION.

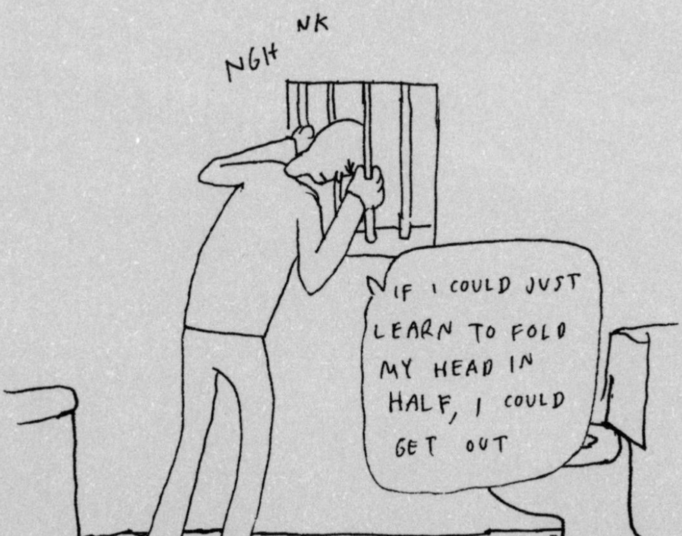
NGH
NK
IF I COULD JUST LEARN TO FOLD MY HEAD IN HALF, I COULD GET OUT

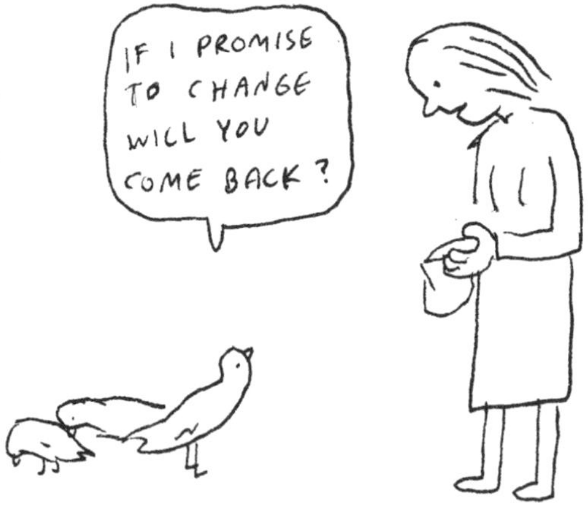
IF I PROMISE TO CHANGE WILL YOU COME BACK?

IT JUST HASN'T BEEN THE SAME SINCE YOU LEFT

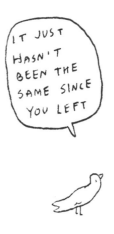

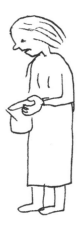

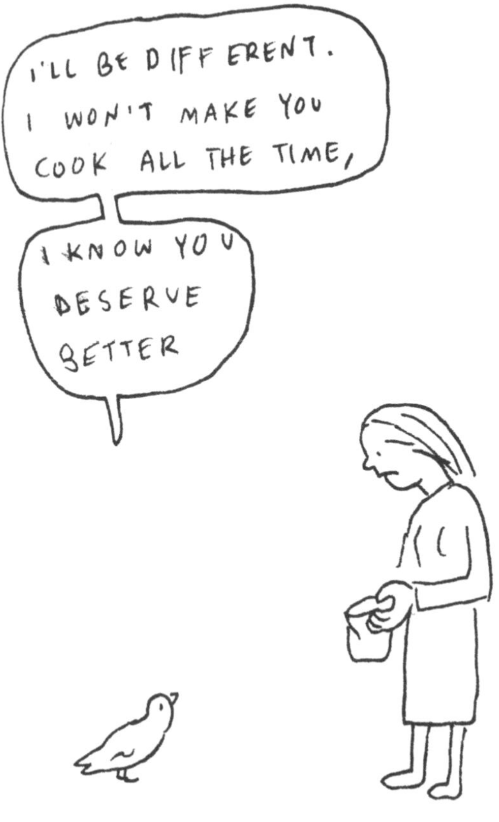
I'LL BE DIFFERENT. I WON'T MAKE YOU COOK ALL THE TIME,
I KNOW YOU DESERVE BETTER

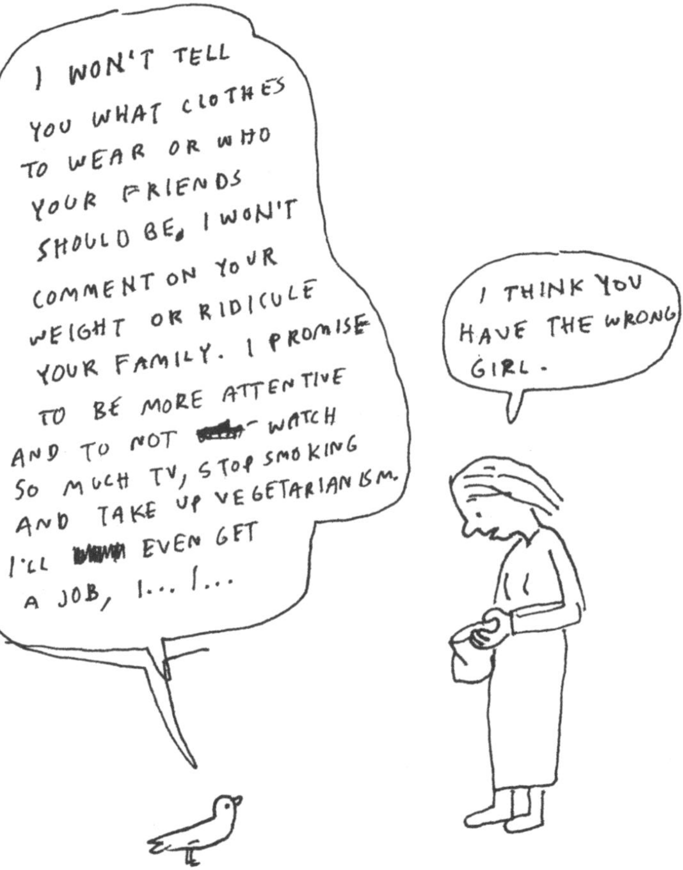

YOU'RE NOT SUSAN MCDOUGAL OF 135 JANSPORT LANE?
NO

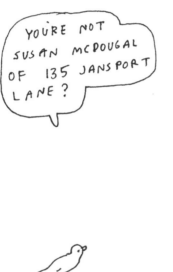

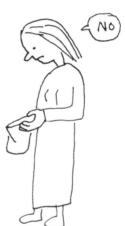

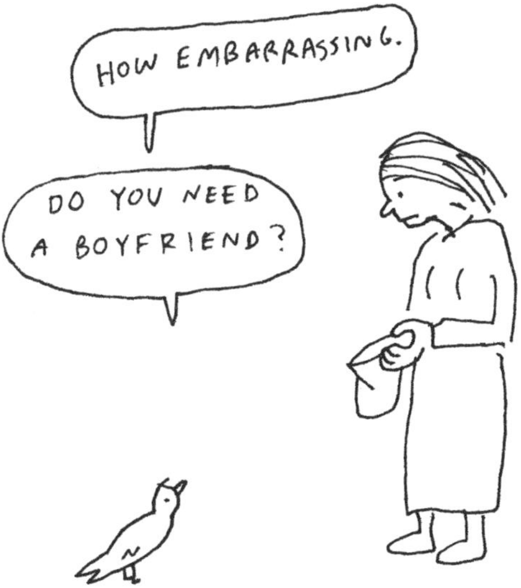
HOW EMBARRASSING.
DO YOU NEED A BOYFRIEND?

the wilderness

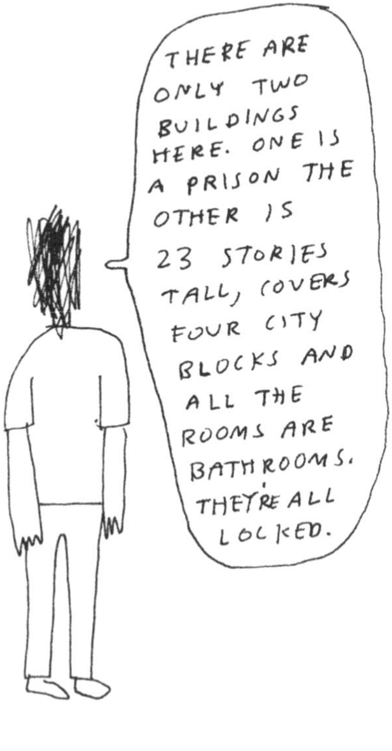
THERE ARE ONLY TWO BUILDINGS HERE. ONE IS A PRISON THE OTHER IS 23 STORIES TALL, COVERS FOUR CITY BLOCKS AND ALL THE ROOMS ARE BATHROOMS. THEY'RE ALL LOCKED.

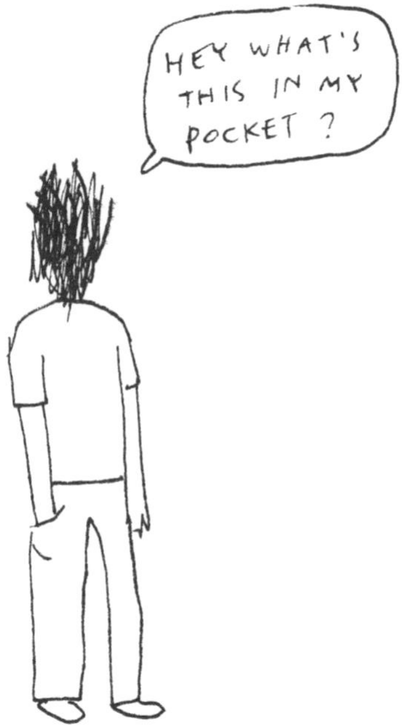
HEY WHAT'S THIS IN MY POCKET ?

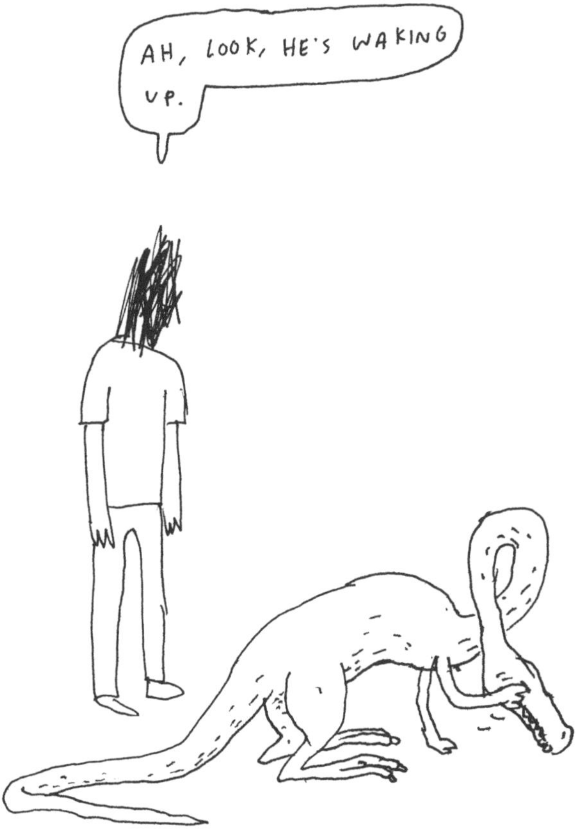
AH, LOOK, HE'S WAKING UP.

HOW ARE YOU FEELING, FRIEND? STILL HUNG OVER?
?

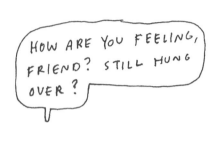

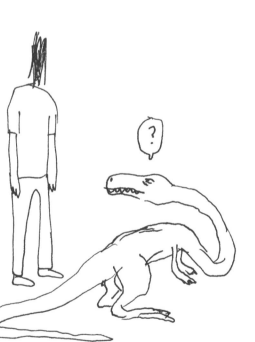

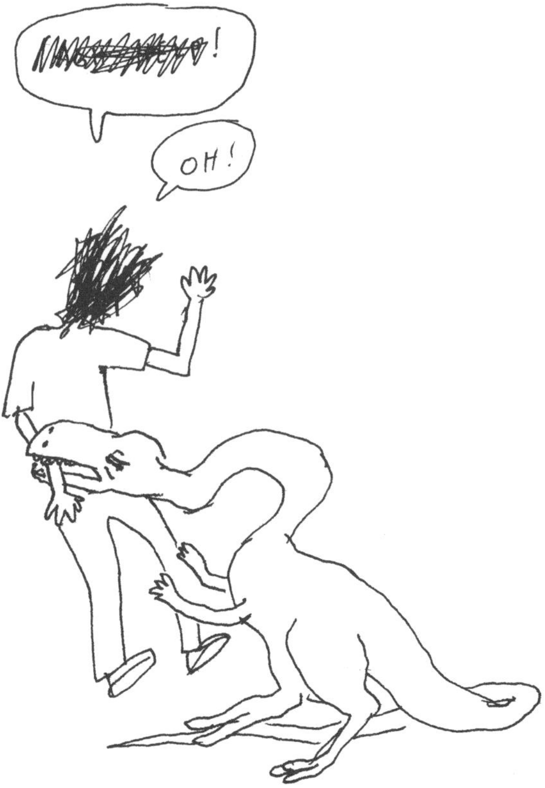
OH!

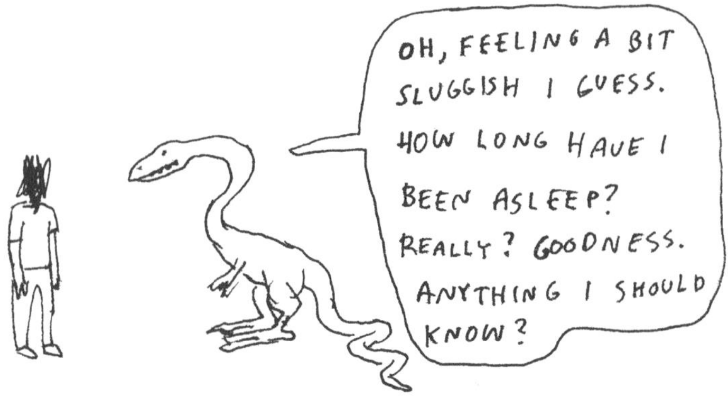
OH, FEELING A BIT SLUGGISH I GUESS. HOW LONG HAVE I BEEN ASLEEP? REALLY? GOODNESS. ANYTHING I SHOULD KNOW?

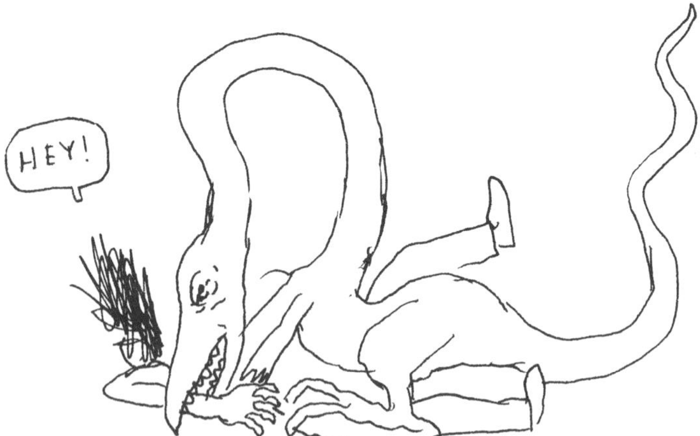
HEY!

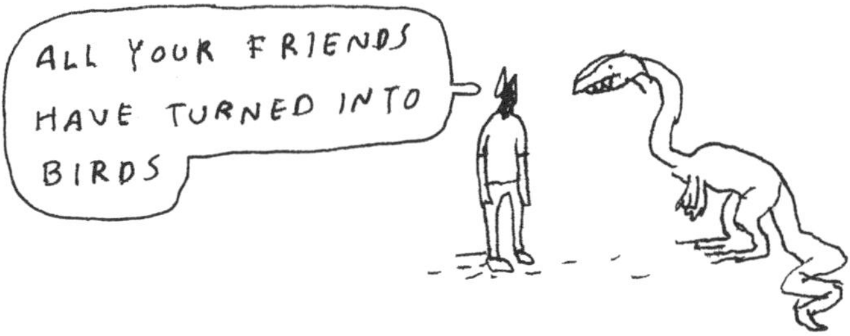
ALL YOUR FRIENDS HAVE TURNED INTO BIRDS

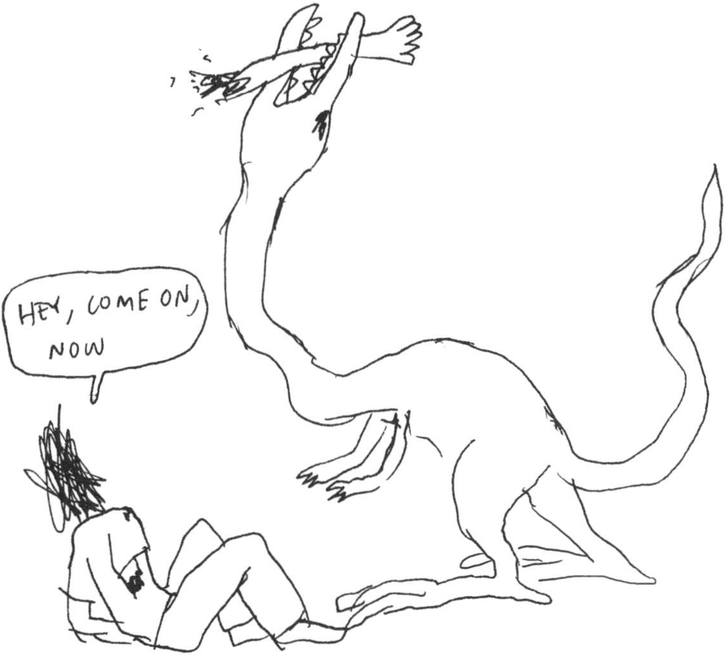
HEY, COME ON, NOW

LATER

WHACK
WHACK
WHACK

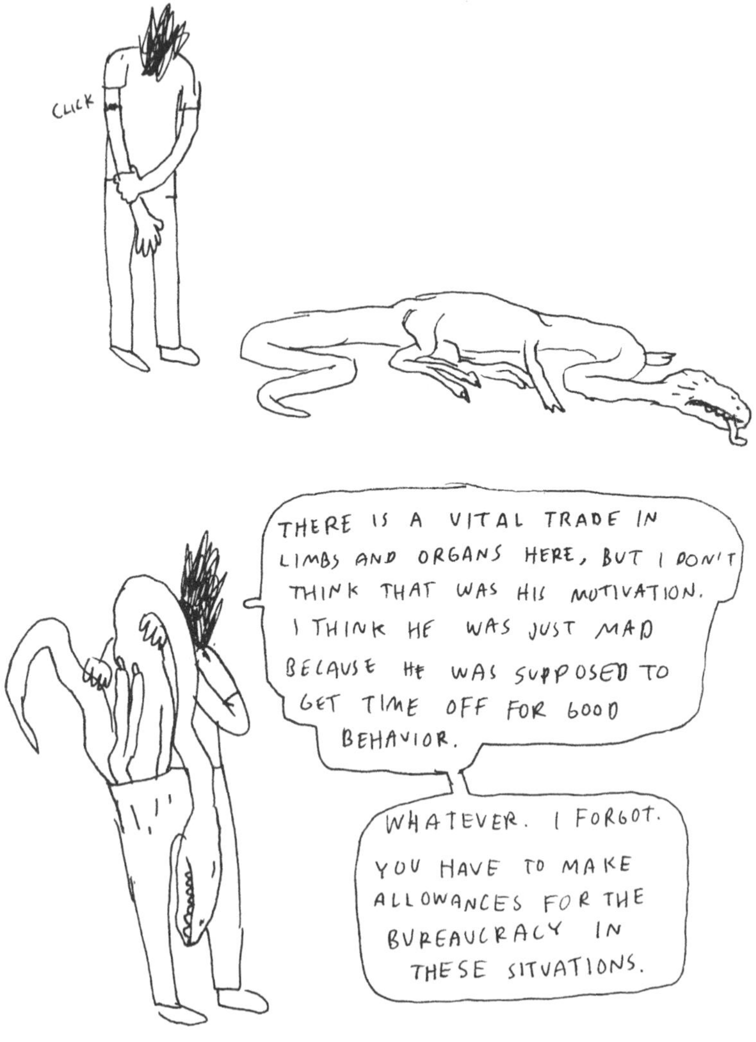
CLICK
THERE IS A VITAL TRADE IN LIMBS AND ORGANS HERE, BUT I DON'T THINK THAT WAS HIS MOTIVATION. I THINK HE WAS JUST MAD BECAUSE HE WAS SUPPOSED TO GET TIME OFF FOR GOOD BEHAVIOR.
WHATEVER. I FORGOT. YOU HAVE TO MAKE ALLOWANCES FOR THE BUREAUCRACY IN THESE SITUATIONS.

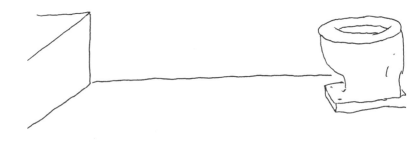

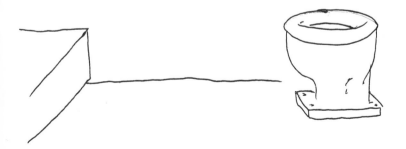

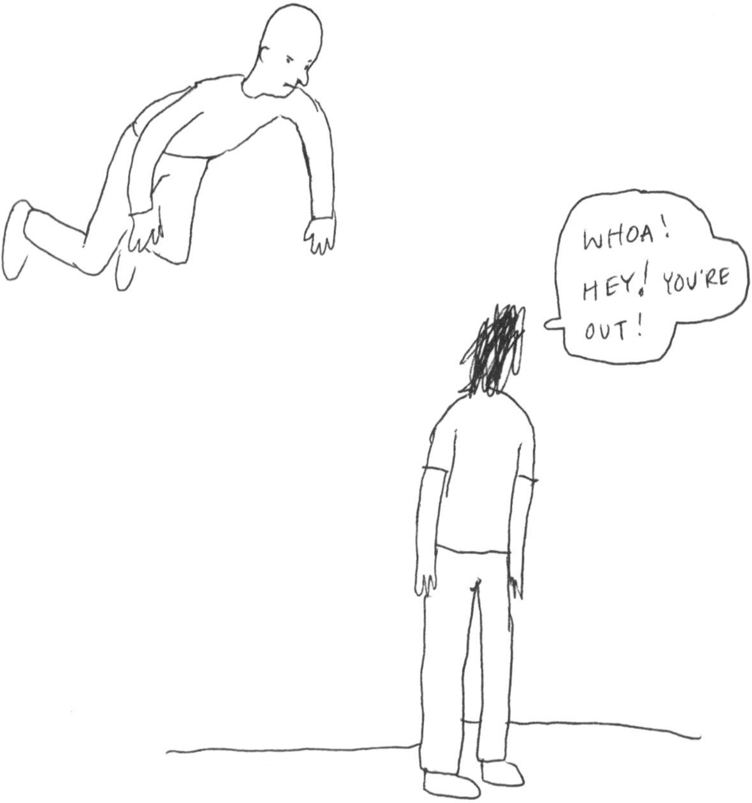
WHOA! HEY! YOU'RE OUT!

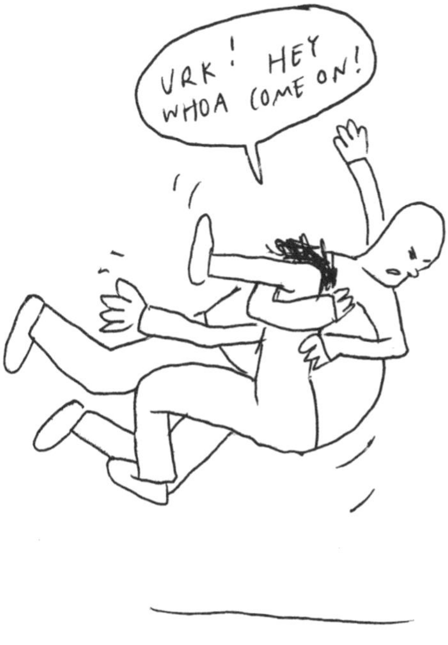
URK! HEY WHOA COME ON!

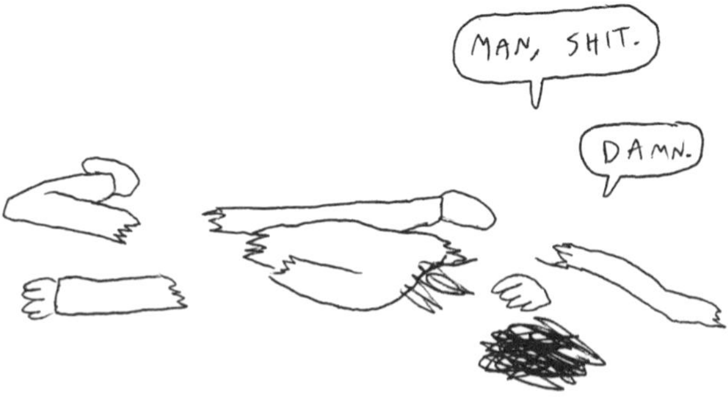
MAN, SHIT.
DAMN.

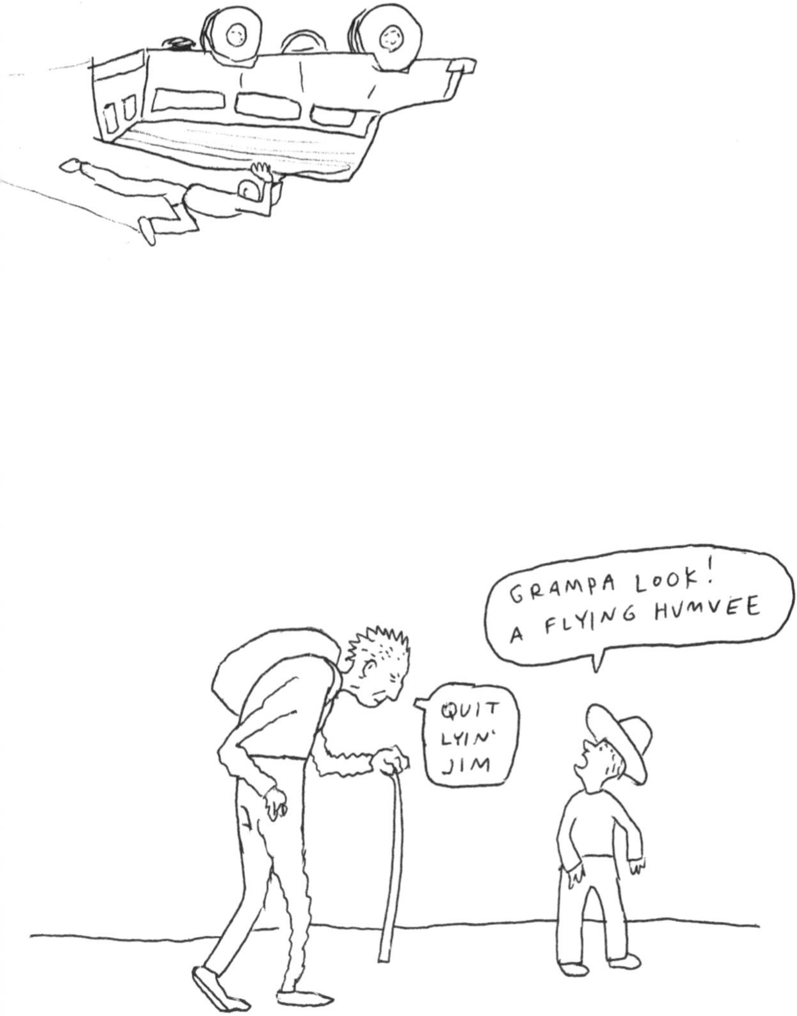
GRAMPA LOOK! A FLYING HUMVEE
QUIT LYIN' JIM

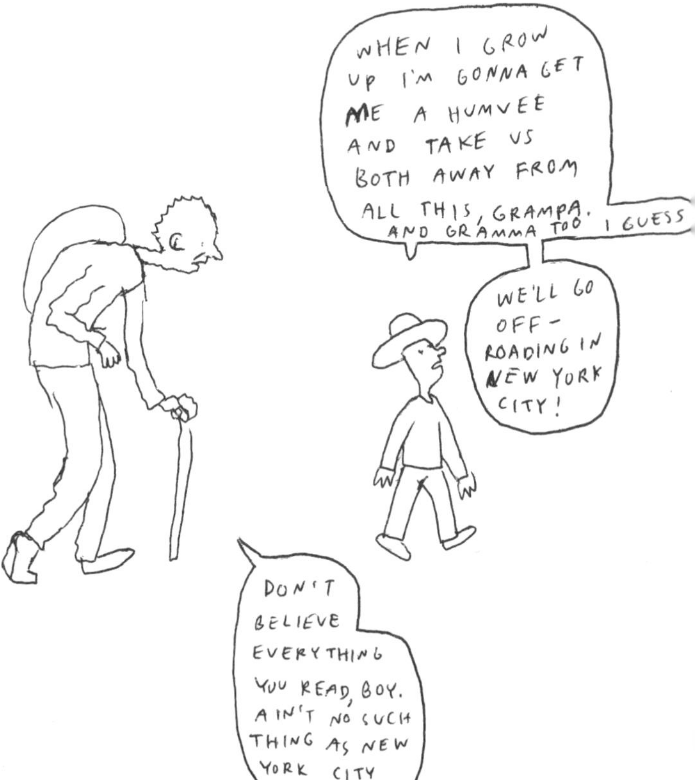

WHEN I GROW UP I'M GONNA GET ME A HUMVEE AND TAKE US BOTH AWAY FROM ALL THIS, GRAMPA. AND GRAMMA TOO I GUESS
WE'LL GO OFF-ROADING IN NEW YORK CITY!
DON'T BELIEVE EVERYTHING YOU READ, BOY. AIN'T NO SUCH THING AS NEW YORK CITY

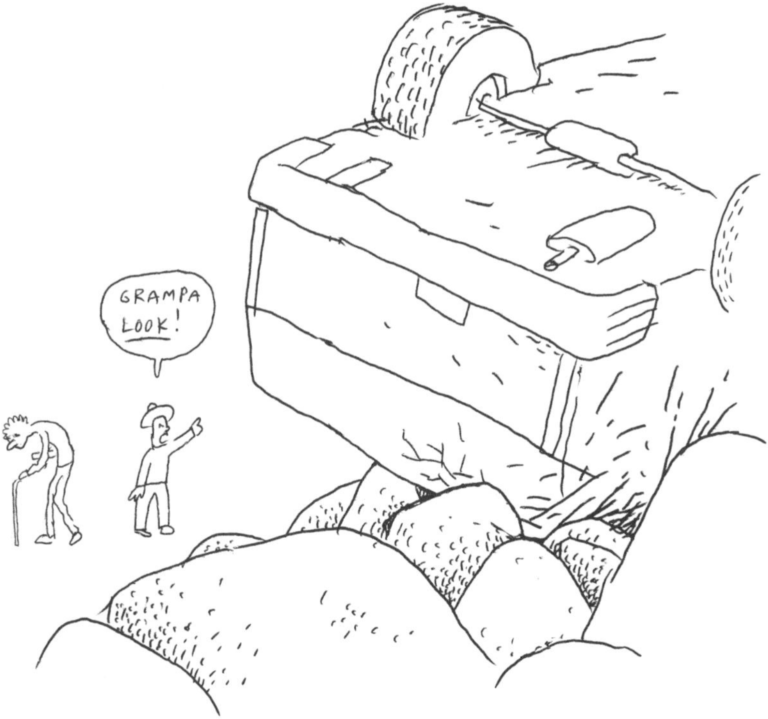
GRAMPA LOOK!

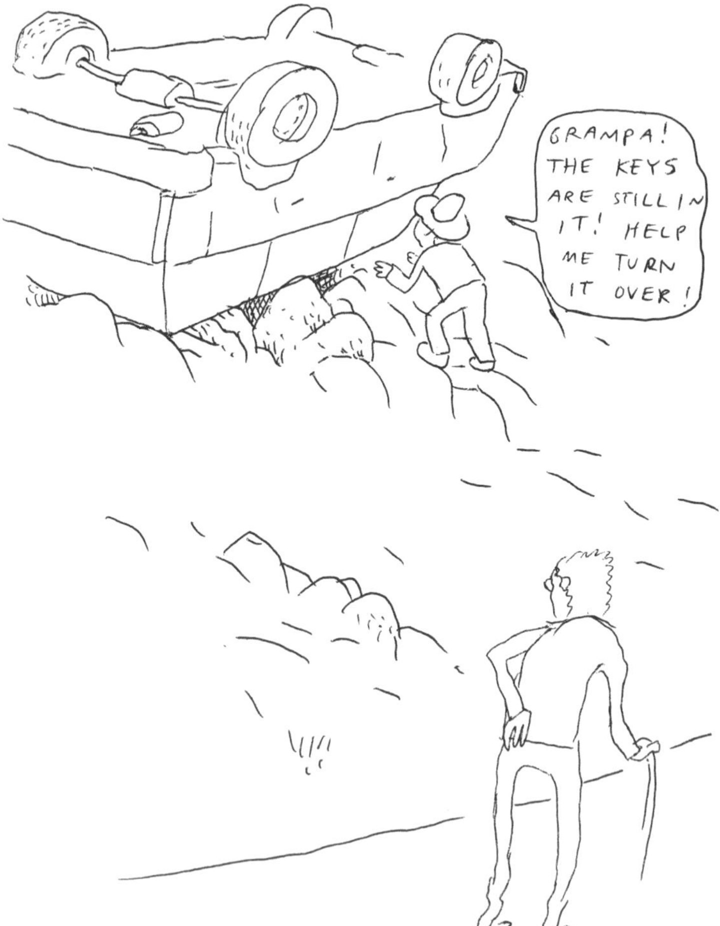
GRAMPA! THE KEYS ARE STILL IN IT! HELP ME TURN IT OVER!

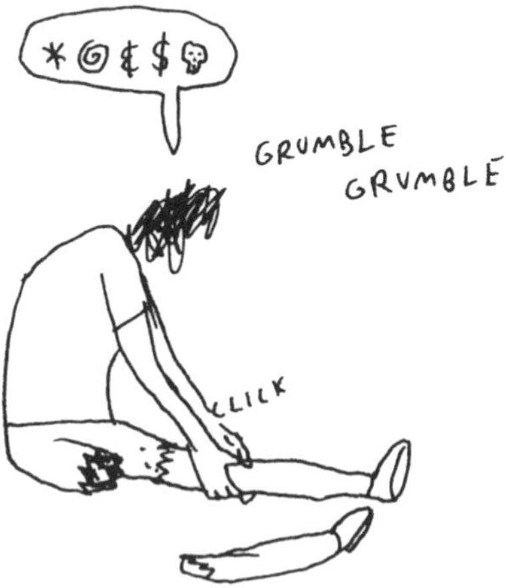
*@¢$
GRUMBLE
GRUMBLE
CLICK

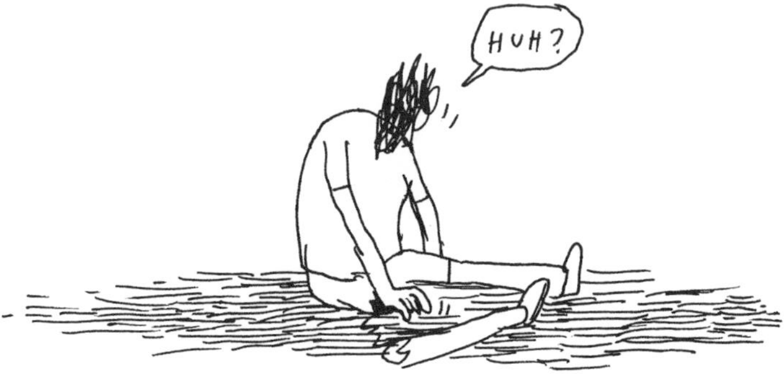
HUH?

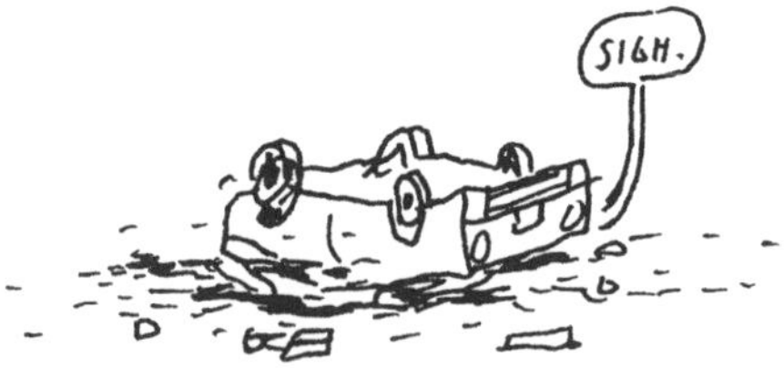
SIGH.

the wilderness part 2

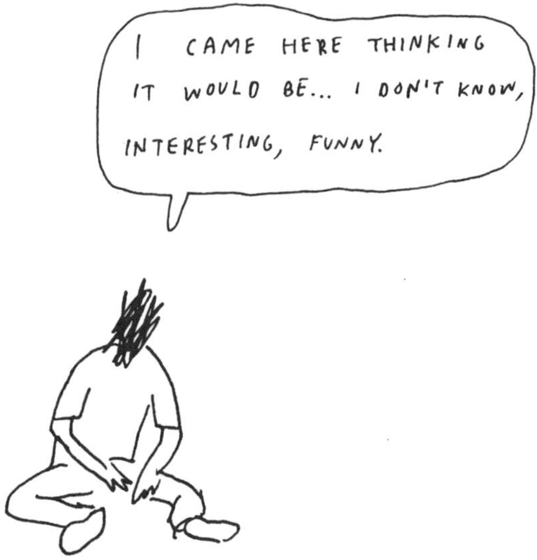
I CAME HERE THINKING IT WOULD BE... I DON'T KNOW, INTERESTING, FUNNY.

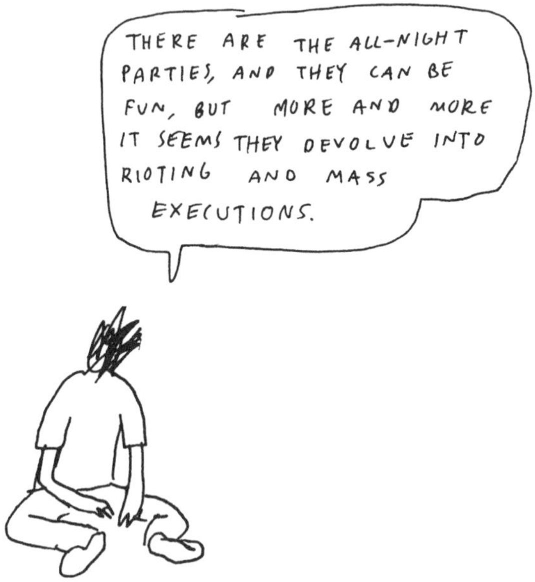
THERE ARE THE ALL-NIGHT PARTIES, AND THEY CAN BE FUN, BUT MORE AND MORE IT SEEMS THEY DEVOLVE INTO RIOTING AND MASS EXECUTIONS.

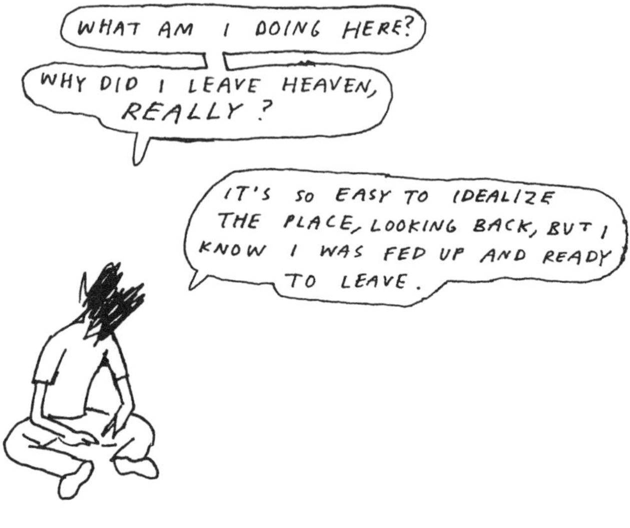
WHAT AM I DOING HERE?
WHY DID I LEAVE HEAVEN, REALLY?
IT'S SO EASY TO IDEALIZE THE PLACE, LOOKING BACK, BUT I KNOW I WAS FED UP AND READY TO LEAVE.

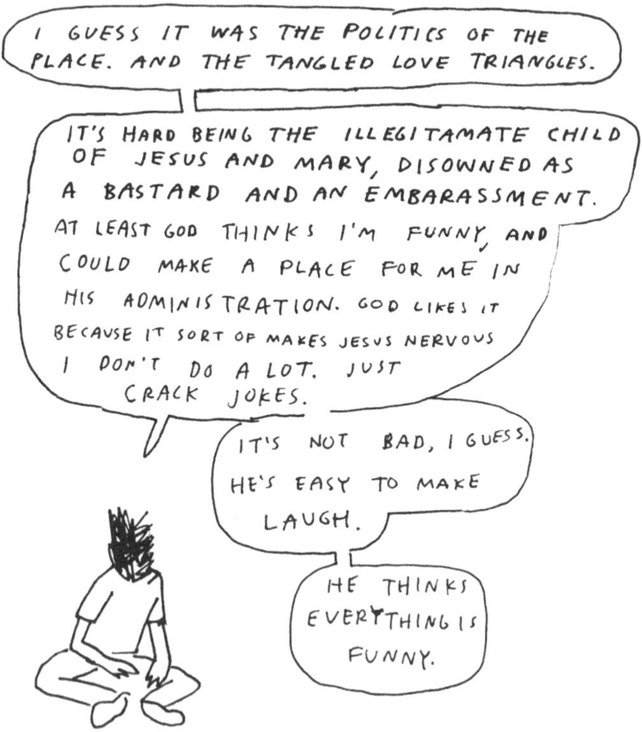
I GUESS IT WAS THE POLITICS OF THE PLACE. AND THE TANGLED LOVE TRIANGLES.
IT'S HARD BEING THE ILLEGITAMATE CHILD OF JESUS AND MARY, DISOWNED AS A BASTARD AND AN EMBARASSMENT. AT LEAST GOD THINKS I'M FUNNY, AND COULD MAKE A PLACE FOR ME IN HIS ADMINISTRATION. GOD LIKES IT BECAUSE IT SORT OF MAKES JESUS NERVOUS I DON'T DO A LOT. JUST CRACK JOKES.
IT'S NOT BAD, I GUESS. HE'S EASY TO MAKE LAUGH.
HE THINKS EVERYTHING IS FUNNY.

BUT JOSEPH WAS ALWAYS KIND OF HARD ON ME. OF COURSE HE DOESN'T HAVE A PROBLEM WITH **GOD**, EVEN GIVEN THAT WHOLE PATERNITY ISSUE. NEITHER ONE OF THEM IS REALLY THE JEALOUS TYPE, BUT FOR JOSEPH I GUESS I'M KIND OF HARD TO IGNORE. OBVIOUSLY GOD'S NOT GOING TO FEEL THREATENED BY JOSEPH, WHO WAS REALLY ONLY EVEN MADE A SAINT AS A FORMALITY. BUT THEN, NOBODY REALLY TALKS TO HIM ABOUT THE FINE POINTS EITHER. HE ACTUALLY STILL PRETTY MUCH THINKS THE WHOLE "SON OF GOD" THING IS, AS HE SAYS, "FIGURATIVE"

HEH HEH

GOD THINKS THAT'S JUST HILARIOUS.

IT HAD JUST BEEN A LONG
TIME... IT FELT LIKE, YOU KNOW,
TIME TO GET AWAY.

I THOUGHT A LITTLE
TIME IN THE WILDERNESS WOULD
BE A NICE DIVERSION.
WOULD KEEP ME OCCUPIED.

MAYBE I COULD MEET NEW PEOPLE...
IT JUST SEEMED MORE REAL.

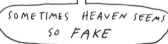

SOMETIMES HEAVEN SEEMS
SO FAKE

I'M NOT SURE IT'S WORKING OUT, THOUGH

LIKE, MY AUNT, WHO SORT OF RUNS THE PLACE
SHE'S ALL RIGHT. BUT SOMETIMES YOU
GET THE FEELING, WHEN YOU'RE
TALKING TO HER, SHE'S NOT **REALLY**
LISTENING. SHE NEVER SEEMS TO
QUITE LOOK AT YOU.

OF COURSE IT'S
HARD TO TELL IN
A WAY, BECAUSE HER
HEAD'S ON FIRE.

I DON'T
KNOW...

NOBODY SEEMS
TO REALLY GET
MY SENSE OF
HUMOR HERE.

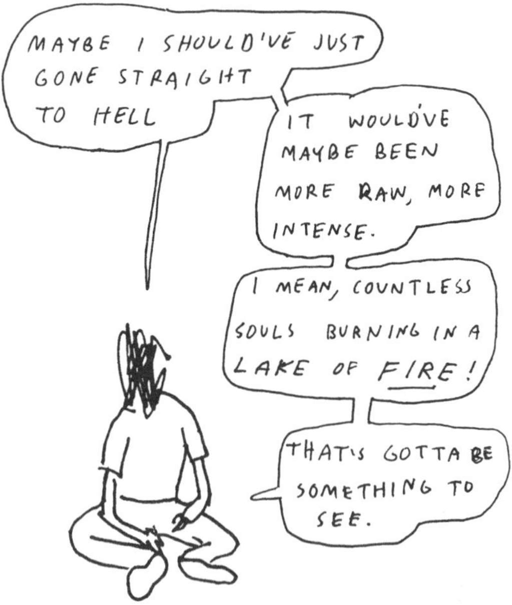
MAYBE I SHOULD'VE JUST GONE STRAIGHT TO HELL
IT WOULD'VE MAYBE BEEN MORE RAW, MORE INTENSE.
I MEAN, COUNTLESS SOULS BURNING IN A LAKE OF FIRE!
THAT'S GOTTA BE SOMETHING TO SEE.

I DON'T KNOW, THOUGH. I'VE NEVER REALLY GOTTEN ALONG WITH LUCIFER.
HE'S JUST ALWAYS SO SERIOUS.
WHAT A DRAG.

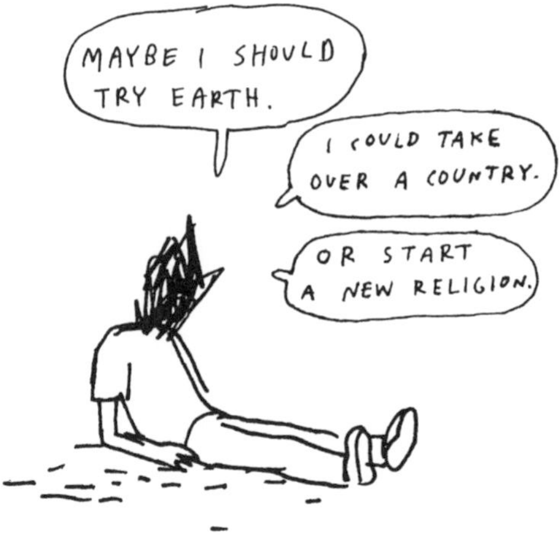
MAYBE I SHOULD TRY EARTH.
I COULD TAKE OVER A COUNTRY.
OR START A NEW RELIGION.

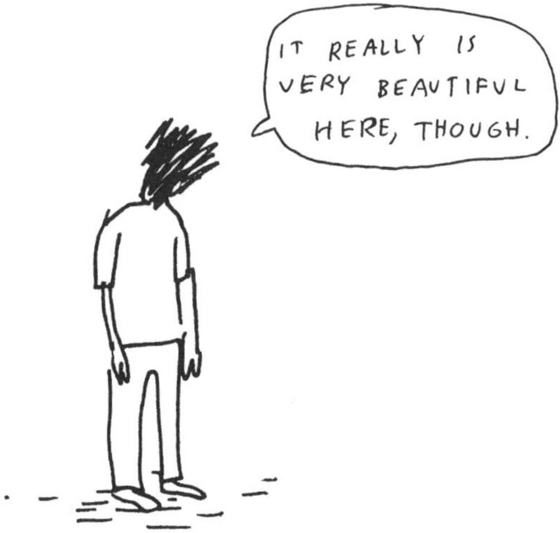
IT REALLY IS VERY BEAUTIFUL HERE, THOUGH.

YAWN

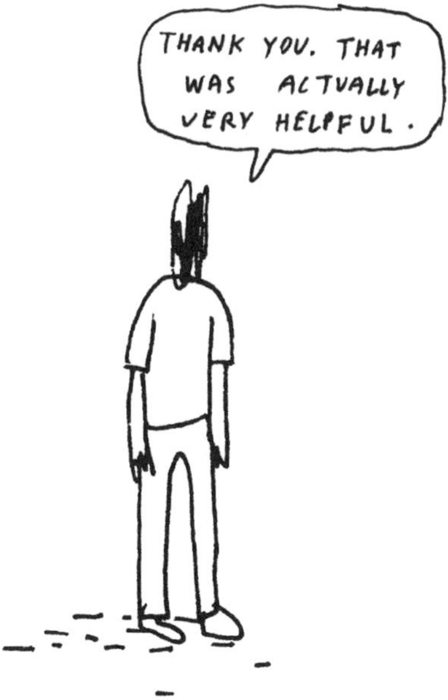
THANK YOU. THAT WAS ACTUALLY VERY HELPFUL.

the mediocrity principle

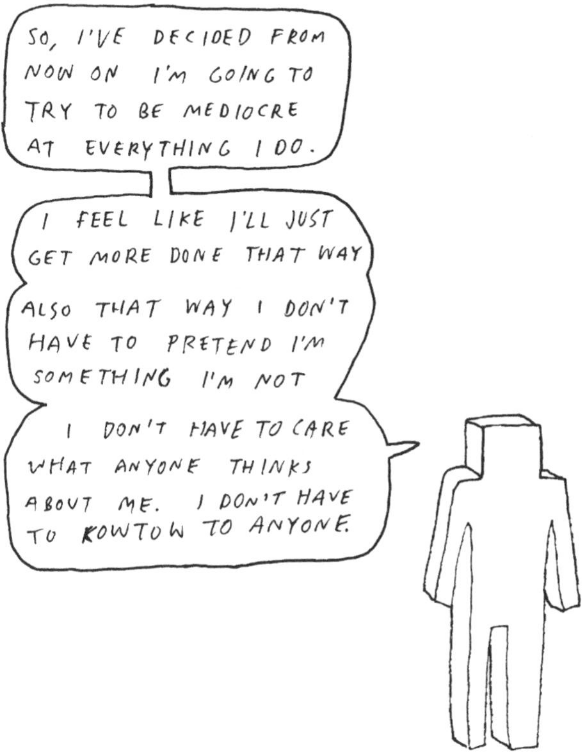
SO, I'VE DECIDED FROM NOW ON I'M GOING TO TRY TO BE MEDIOCRE AT EVERYTHING I DO.
I FEEL LIKE I'LL JUST GET MORE DONE THAT WAY
ALSO THAT WAY I DON'T HAVE TO PRETEND I'M SOMETHING I'M NOT
I DON'T HAVE TO CARE WHAT ANYONE THINKS ABOUT ME. I DON'T HAVE TO KOWTOW TO ANYONE.

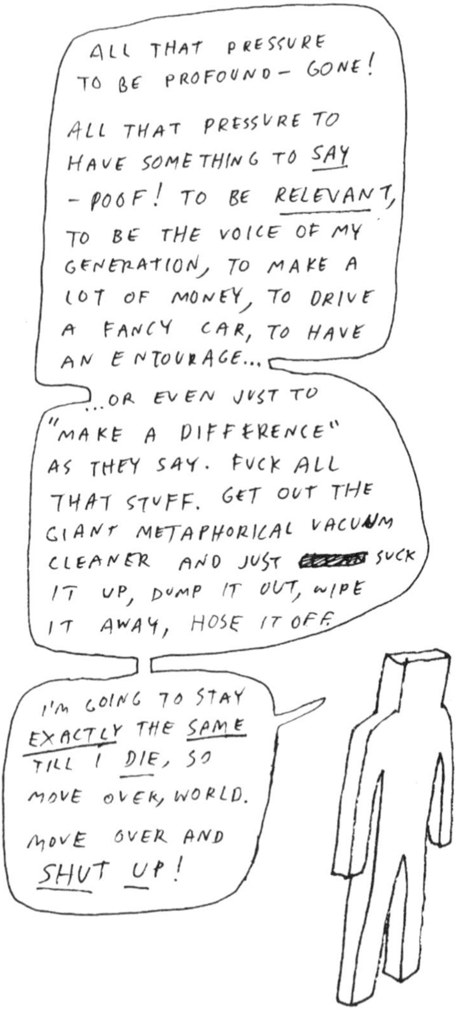

THAT PRESSURE TO ENGAGE, TO BREAK OUT OF ONE'S HABITS...

I LIKE MY HABITS. I DON'T NEED TO CHALLENGE ANYONE, LEAST OF ALL MYSELF. I'M FINE JUST THE WAY I AM.

AND IF I NEED TO I'LL START SUCKING. IF IT COMES TO THAT, FINE. THAT'S HOW FAR I'M WILLING TO GO WITH THIS!

NO LIMITS!

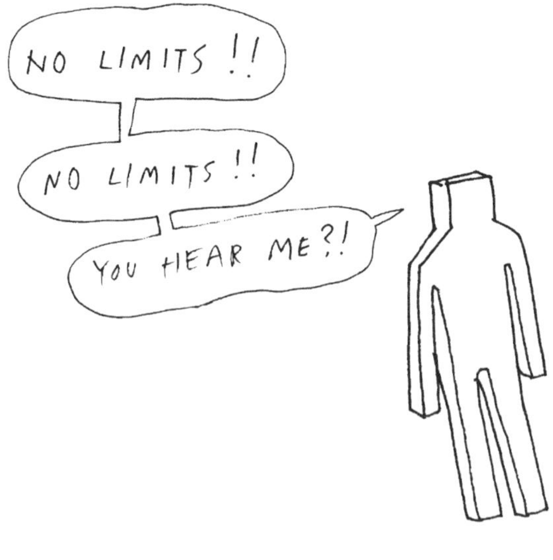
NO LIMITS !!
NO LIMITS !!
YOU HEAR ME?!

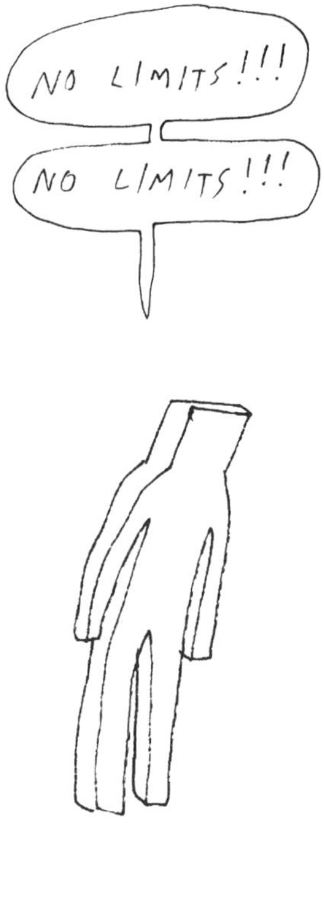
NO LIMITS!!!
NO LIMITS!!!

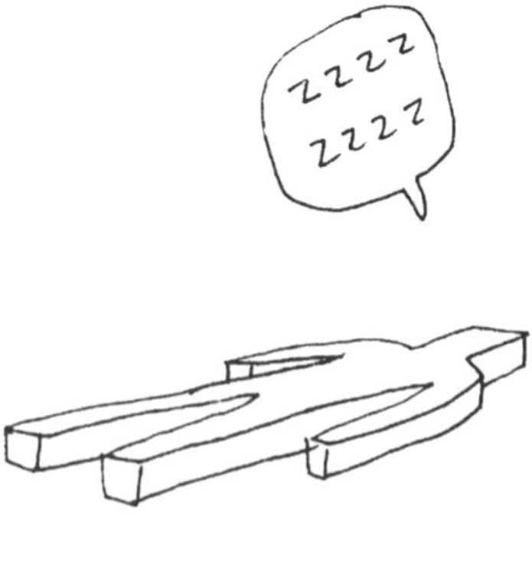
zzzz
zzzz

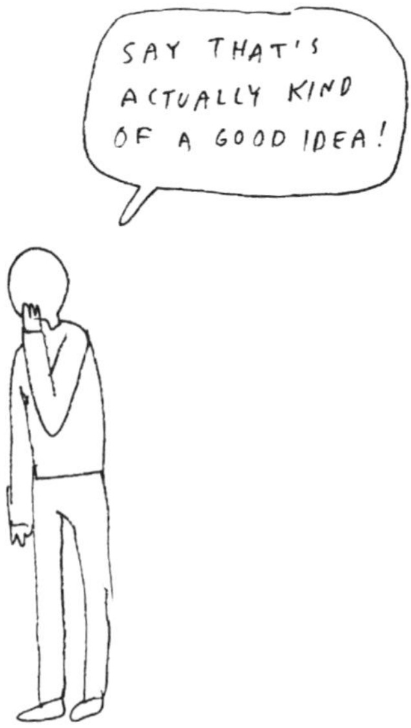
SAY THAT'S ACTUALLY KIND OF A GOOD IDEA!

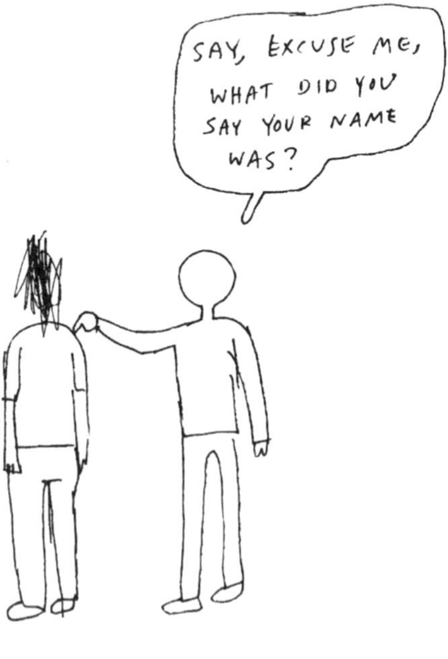
SAY, EXCUSE ME, WHAT DID YOU SAY YOUR NAME WAS?

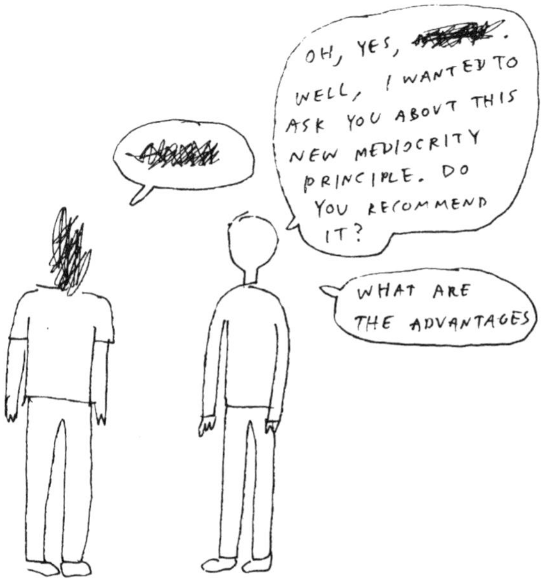
[redacted]
OH, YES, [redacted]. WELL, I WANTED TO ASK YOU ABOUT THIS NEW MEDIOCRITY PRINCIPLE. DO YOU RECOMMEND IT?
WHAT ARE THE ADVANTAGES

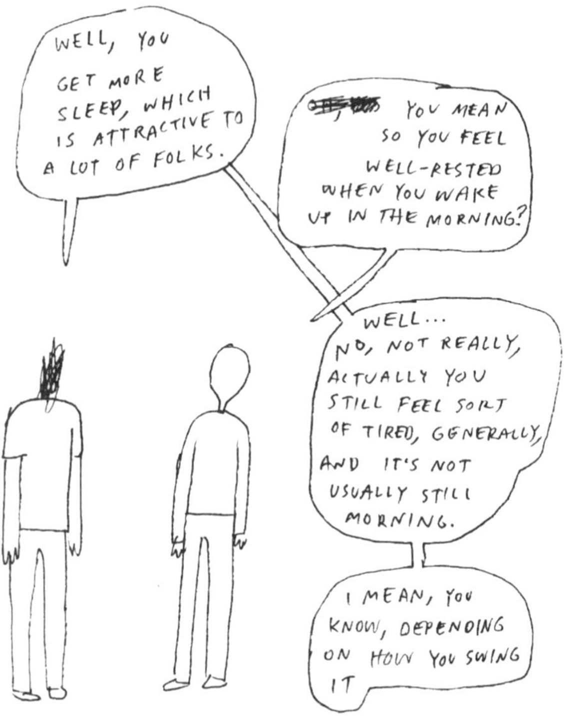
WELL, YOU GET MORE SLEEP, WHICH IS ATTRACTIVE TO A LOT OF FOLKS.
YOU MEAN SO YOU FEEL WELL-RESTED WHEN YOU WAKE UP IN THE MORNING?
WELL... NO, NOT REALLY, ACTUALLY YOU STILL FEEL SORT OF TIRED, GENERALLY, AND IT'S NOT USUALLY STILL MORNING.
I MEAN, YOU KNOW, DEPENDING ON HOW YOU SWING IT

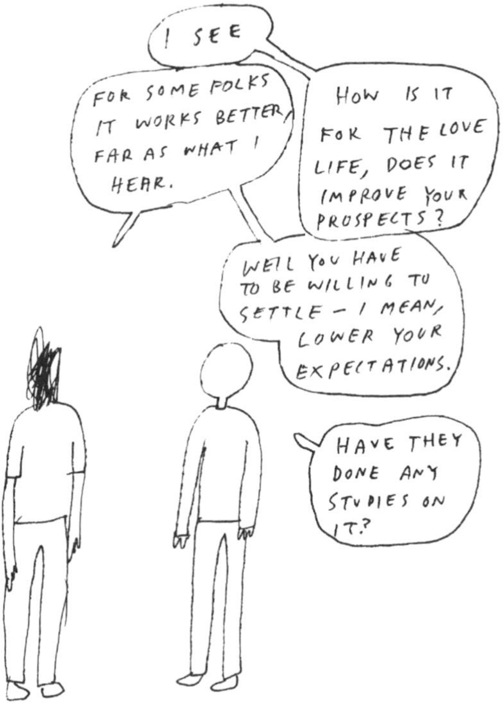
I SEE
FOR SOME FOLKS IT WORKS BETTER, FAR AS WHAT I HEAR.
HOW IS IT FOR THE LOVE LIFE, DOES IT IMPROVE YOUR PROSPECTS?
WELL YOU HAVE TO BE WILLING TO SETTLE - I MEAN, LOWER YOUR EXPECTATIONS.
HAVE THEY DONE ANY STUDIES ON IT?

NOT YET, IT'S STILL A NEW PHENOMENON AND IT'S NOT EXPECTED TO LAST. THEY MAY DO SOME STUDIES IN THE FUTURE THOUGH, WOULD YOU LIKE ME TO CHECK?

OH YES, IF YOU DON'T MIND.

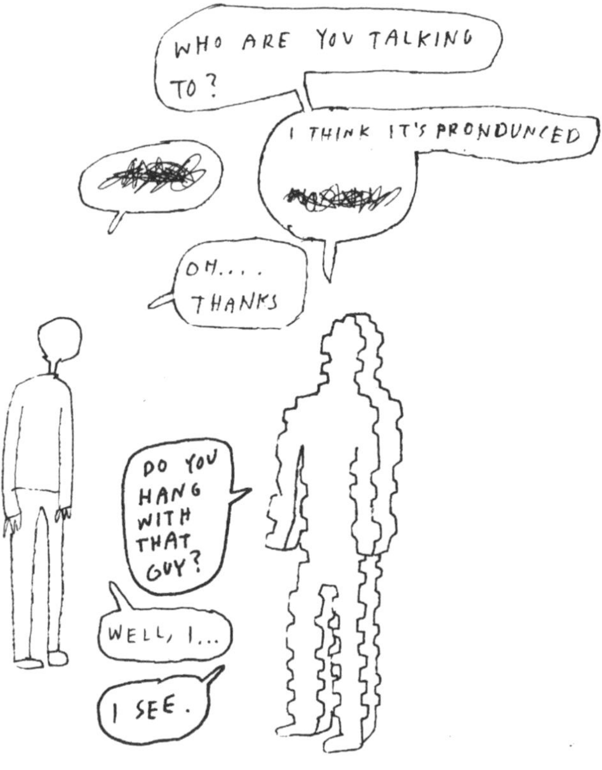
WHO ARE YOU TALKING TO?
I THINK IT'S PRONDUNCED
OH.... THANKS
DO YOU HANG WITH THAT GUY?
WELL, I...
I SEE.

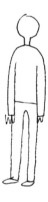

WELL I FOUND SOMETHING.
IT SAYS IT'S ASSOCIATED WITH ATROPHYING.
ATROPHYING ? ATROPHYING WHAT? WHAT ATROPHIES? LIKE YOUR BRAIN? OR THE SEX ORGANS OR WHAT?
I DON'T KNOW, I COULDN'T GET A CLEAR PICTURE.
I GUESS YOU GOTTA TAKE YOUR CHANCES.
IT'S SUPER HARD TO DO STUDIES IN THE FUTURE

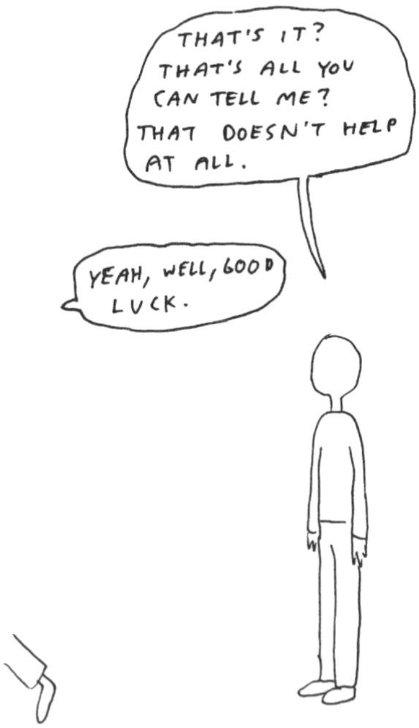
THAT'S IT? THAT'S ALL YOU CAN TELL ME? THAT DOESN'T HELP AT ALL.
YEAH, WELL, GOOD LUCK.

next:

I'M ACTUALLY NOT ME.

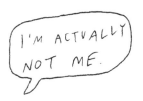

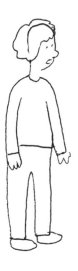

appendix

MIA FARROW: I HOPE YOU DON'T READ MY BOOK

DAVID LETTERMAN: OH REALLY? WHY'S THAT?

MIA : WELL WE HAVE SUCH A NICE SIMPLE
      TV RELATIONSHIP HERE I WOULDN'T
      WANT ~~ME~~ TO HAVE YOU FIND OUT
      HOW I REALLY AM AND RUIN THAT.
      THIS IS THE BEST RELATIONSHIP
      IN MY LIFE.

DAVID : YEAH. I CAN RELATE TO THAT.

THIS BOOK IS DEDICATED TO
TO EVERYONE WHO CAME ON THE KRAMERS TOUR:
PARTICULARLY SAMMY, SOUTHER, LAUREN, DAVID, RON
AND JOSH. IN ADDITION TO THEM THIS BOOK, AND EVERYTHING
I DO FOR THE NEXT HUNDRED THOUSAND YEARS, IS FOR,
ABOVE ALL, CHERYL.

A COUPLE OF OTHER THINGS: ~~█████████~~
THE WILDERNESS, PART 2 ORIGINALLY APPEARED
IN KRAMER'S ERGOT #5, THE MEDIOCRITY PRINCIPLE
FIRST APPEARED IN BLOOD ORANGE #3 AND WAS
EXCERPTED IN 'BEST AMERICAN NON-REQUIRED READING
2005'. JOB HUNT FIRST APPEARED IN THE CHICAGO
READER YEAR END ISSUE, 2003
        THE TWO SECTIONS OF THE BOOK, INDICATED BY THE
TWO PAPER STOCKS, REPRESENT THE FACT THAT THIS
VOLUME COMPRISES TWO CONSECUTIVE SKETCHBOOKS...THE
FIRST WITH ROUGH BROWN PAPER (SOME REMNANTS STILL
VISIBLE). THE DIVISION OF MATERIAL HERE IS NOT
EXACT. I MOVED THINGS AROUND A LITTLE FOR
THE SAKE OF CONTINUITY.

ANDERS NILSEN 1-10-06

contact: Anders Nilsen 3103 W. Augusta Blvd, Chicago, Il 60622
or ndrs@hotmail.com
Fantagraphics Books 7563 Lake City Way NE, Seattle WA, 98115
Published by Gary Groth and Kim Thompson

ISBN-13: 978-1-56097-718-6
ISBN-10: 1-56097-718-3

Printed in Singapore